W9-BXM-622

Writing Short Stories for Young People

WRITING SHORT STORIES FOR YOUNG PEOPLE

George Edward Stanley

Writer's
Digest
Books

Cincinnati, Ohio

Writing Short Stories for Young People. Copyright © 1986 by George Edward Stanley. Printed and bound in the United States of America. All rights reserved. No part of this book may be reproduced in any form or by any electronic or mechanical means including information storage and retrieval systems without permission in writing from the publisher, except by a reviewer, who may quote brief passages in a review. Published by Writer's Digest Books, an imprint of F&W Publications, Inc., 1507 Dana Avenue, Cincinnati, Ohio 45207. First edition.
Second printing, 1987

Library of Congress Cataloging-in-Publication Data

Stanley, George Edward.
Writing short stories for young people.

1. Children's stories—Authorship. I. Title.
PN3377.S73   1987   808.06'831   86-28928
ISBN 0-89879-256-8

Design by Joan Ann Jacobus

To
Gwen
and to
James and Charles,
with all my love

Acknowledgments

This book grew out of a relationship with the Saturday Evening Post Youth Publications/Children's Better Health Institute that began in 1977 and continues today. Through the years, I have written many stories and developed several series for the various magazines of this group. I have also made many friends: Peg Rogers, John Craton, Ray Randolph, William Wagner, Steve Charles, Julie Plopper, and Beth Wood Thomas. Thank you all very much!

During all stages of the writing of this book, I have been extremely fortunate to have the support and incredible editorial expertise of the people at Writer's Digest Books: Howard I. Wells III, Jean Fredette, Carol Cartaino, David E. Lewis, and especially Nancy A. Dibble.

Many, many friends have supported me in this effort, especially Sue Alexander, James Cross Giblin, Ellen E. Krieger, Joan Lowery Nixon, Dian Curtis Regan, and Barbara Seuling.

I want to thank my colleagues at Cameron University, Dr. Josephine Raburn, Head of the Division of Language Arts; Dr. Charles Smith, Vice-President for Academics; and Dr. Don Davis, President; for their continued support of both my writing and of the university's professional writing program.

I want to thank my colleagues at the Institute of Children's Literature for their interest and support, especially Joan Gozzi and Pamela Kelly.

I want to thank my agent and friend, Susan Cohen, at Writer's House, whose faith in me has been a sustaining force.

And finally, I want to thank my family, all of them, for their support throughout the years.

Contents

Part Three

PUTTING IT ALL TOGETHER

Part One

You and the World of Young People's Stories

1

Writing and Writing for Young People

There are all kinds of reasons that people want to write for young people. Before you read any further, I wish you'd be very honest with yourself and determine why it is that you're really doing what you're doing—reading a book that will tell you how to write and publish short stories for young people. I want you to take a test for me. When you finish this test, you'll know whether or not you really want to write for young people.

TEST

1. You're at a meeting and some teenage girls come in and sit down. They have their heads together and they're giggling and whispering and talking, all at the same time. Then they get up and

2

leave the room, continuing to giggle and whisper and talk. Do you think:

> A. *What a bunch of silly teenage girls!*

> B. *I know exactly what they're thinking. It seems like only yesterday that I was doing the same thing.*

2. You're trying to teach a bunch of boys how to do something, but all they're interested in doing is talking about sports and shoving each other around. Do you think:

> A. *If they can't listen to me, then they can just get somebody else to work with this bunch of idiots!*

> B. *I found it hard to sit still when I was their age, too, so I'll get through this lesson as best I can and then we'll do a physical activity.*

3. Your son has returned from a field trip with some broken toys, an old bottle, and a "metal-looking" thing. Do you say to him:

> A. *You're not going to bring that junk into this house. You don't know what kind of germs it has on it!*

> B. *Those things could be valuable. Let's look at them closely and find a good place to keep them.*

4. Your daughter has decided she wants to be an entomologist when she grows up, so she starts bringing bugs into the house. Do you say:

> A. *Take those dirty things back outside!*

> B. *Those look like fascinating creatures. Let's find something we can put them in so we can observe them.*

5. Your son tells you he wants to have a horse more than anything else in the world. Do you say:

> A. *Where in the world would we get the money for a*

horse, and besides, where do you think we'd keep it?

B. *Well, they're awfully expensive, but we'll look into how much one would cost and where we could keep it.*

6. Your daughter has just told you she wants to build a treehouse. Do you think:

A. *She'll kill the tree.*

B. *I remember the excitement of being above the leaves and looking down in wonder at my kingdom below.*

You may now be thinking, *What an easy test! I know which answers I should choose!* The point is that you shouldn't have chosen the answers that you *knew* would give you a high score on the test but those that truthfully represent how you would feel in the different situations. Of course, all the "A" answers represent the wrong attitude, while all the "B" answers represent the right attitude. Now, I'd be less than honest if I told you that in all cases my attitude was that of the "B" responses, but I *generally* respond according to the "B" responses in most of the situations I've described. From this test, you can readily see that much of writing for young people is in your attitude toward young people and what they do.

No matter what you think or have been told, writing is hard work, and writing for young people is especially hard. There are a lot of people out there waiting to see if you succeed or fail: your family, your friends, your fellow workers, editors, other writers. You'd better be serious about all of this before you start writing, because a lot of people are going to be watching you.

Whether or not you realize it, writing for young people carries with it a great responsibility. Remember, some young person is actually going to read what you've written and be influenced by it. Keeping this in mind can be helpful, because it should make you want to put your best foot forward and produce not only something that you'll be proud of but something that the young reader will never forget, whether it carries a lesson for life or simply re-

4

counts an exciting adventure.

No, it's not easy to write for young people. I'm often amused at beginning writers who tell me that they plan to start out writing something simple for young people, sell to that market for a while, then go on to bigger and better things in the adult market. I usually say very little to them, for they've already made up their minds that it must be very easy to write for young people. I always think it'll be more educational if they find out for themselves just how wrong they are.

Do you have to like young people in order to write for young people? No, I don't think you do, and this is probably going to upset and surprise a lot of readers. Now, I happen to love *my* children, but other children sometimes get on my nerves. Even my children get on my nerves sometimes! What I want to dispel, however, is the notion that all writers of children's literature are Pied Pipers, surrounded by young people all the time. Writers (and editors) don't have to be doting fatherly, motherly, grandfatherly, or grandmotherly types in order to write for young people. Now, I'd be the first to admit that if you're this type, it probably helps rather than hinders, but what's more important—indeed, what's absolutely necessary—is that you *like* what young people do! You must like the way they live their lives. In fact, I suppose, you must still honestly be a young person at heart.

Now, of course, if you do love young people, even just *like* them, it'll be easier to get to know them and how they live their lives (in case it's been so long since you were a young person that you've forgotten!). However, I do have a great many writer-and-editor friends who've been very successful in the field of children's literature, and, although they've never told me in so many words, I don't think they really care for young people to the point that they surround themselves with young people. I do know, however, whether they're remembering their childhoods or not, that they most definitely like what young people do.

It's very important that you perceive yourself to be a young person; this is one of the secrets of writing for young people. You have to live what a young person is living and feel what a young person is feeling. You have to understand a young person's emotions, fears, disappointments, triumphs. You have to understand what it means to score that soccer goal or not to score it. You have to understand what it means to make 100 percent on a spelling quiz. You have to understand what it means not to understand math. You have to understand what it means not to be able to play football, either because you're too small or because your parents won't let you. You have to understand what it means to have to wait for Christmas or for a birthday party or. . . . I'd say you almost have to become the character you're writing about.

My wife and I have children, so we live in a young person's world most of the time. But our own children tend to grow up, while most of us writers for young people don't grow up. They have an affinity for a certain age—usually the age they remember most fondly—and they write for this age group most of the time. I think I'm this way. I prefer the eight-to-twelve age group. This is the time in my childhood that I remember most fondly. Even when my children have outgrown this age-group, I think I'll still be writing for it, because I simply like what I'm doing and the age I'm writing for, and that's enough for me.

If you don't have any children, or if your children are grown and you've been out of touch with what today's young people are doing, then make friends with the neighborhood young people. I'll admit that in the age we're living in now, this sort of thing is more suspect than it once was, but if you can become friends with the parents of the young people, then it's easier to become friends with the young people themselves. You don't have to invite them into your home. What you want to be able to do is visit with them in their own environment, so you can—yes!—study them! You can visit with them on your porch or their porch or in your yard or their yard. You can visit with them in the corridors or the lobby of your apartment building or in the park.

There are also many opportunities for volunteer work with young people. Check your telephone directory for the number of such organizations as Big Brothers/Big Sisters, Boy Scouts, and Girl Scouts. Give them a call and offer your services.

You don't have to do an in-depth interview when you're talking to a young person. What you want to get is a feel for how young people act today, how they think, what language they use, the rhythm of their lives, their spirit. It's this spirit that you must inject into your stories to have them ring true.

If all this personal contact bothers you, don't despair. It's not easy for all of us to be so outgoing, and this is one of the things I think I resent most about what some writers say about writing for young people. We're not all extroverts, and we're not all capable of plunging into such extroverted activities as those associated with most young people. For those of you who aren't extroverts, there are a number of books in your library or in your local bookstore that discuss in detail *everything* a young person does or is expected to do at every age. These books can be very helpful in understanding the age group that you want to write for.

I also think it's important that you read other books written for the young people in the age group you want to write for. Every year, I read nearly 200 books for young people. Some beginning writers think they'll be influenced in the wrong way if they do this: they think they'll end up telling the same story as the author they've just read. Don't worry about that. You're reading in order to get the rhythm of the books for a particular age group. You're reading in order to get a feel for the language, and the behavior patterns, to see how young people act, and how they feel, these sorts of things. In fact, reading what other writers have written is one of the best ways I know to stimulate your own writing. If you have a story you think would be excellent for a young person, but you haven't been able to put it to paper, then it may be because you simply haven't developed the rhythm needed to produce it. Reading other stories for young people can often help bring about this rhythm.

One of the great things about writing for young people is that they're interested in learning about everything. This can't help but inspire the writer to reach greater heights. You'll want to teach young people, to entertain them, to make them read what you've written. It's quite mind-boggling, frankly, to think that a time will come when a young person will come up to you and tell you that he really enjoyed reading your stories.

You should try to have a particular audience in mind when

you're writing a story. In fact, you may have already decided which age group you want to write for. I like writing for the eight-to-twelve age group because this is the period when *everything* seems exciting. It's that golden period between early school and the teenage years, when everything seems to go wrong. You may, however, prefer the preschool years, or you may prefer to tackle the problems of the teenager. You'll often find that the same subjects may be discussed in all age groups, but of course, the audience you choose will dictate how the subject will be handled. You may, for instance, be writing a story about divorce. What you say in your preschool story will not be the same as what you say in a story for the middle years, nor will that be the same as what you say to teenagers.

In the early years, young people are eager to read about what other young people are doing. A story based on the childhood of a famous person always seems to interest them.

As they grow older, young people broaden their interests. In fact, this happens at a much earlier age today than it did for me or probably even for you. Young people are more knowledgeable today. They're more sophisticated. Finding a subject that will interest them will be a challenge for you. But when I start thinking that young people today are becoming awfully jaded, I need only to visit an elementary school classroom to see that they're really still interested in learning about everything.

Older readers prefer stories that have strong characters who overcome obstacles through their own resourcefulness. They want stories about the real world that will show them how others their own age have succeeded in solving similar problems.

Although young people are still eager to learn, it's very important that as a beginning writer, you know that they lose this eagerness quite early. There are many things today that affect this desire to learn. The most important threat is television. I'm not going to preach against television. I love to watch it, but not at the expense of my reading. I've never lost the pleasure of total immersion in a good book. Unfortunately, it's so easy for young people to slip into the habit of watching television instead of reading—and it's so easy for us parents to let them. I'm often guilty of this. I'll get busy doing something, so I'll let our children watch "just one more program." My wife and I have to struggle constantly against doing this. One way I've combatted this in the past is to let my children read or listen to some of my stories. I don't expect criticism from them, although I certainly get it sometimes. But it's a way of making sure that they're reading, a way of doing things together, and a way of continuing to work on a particular story at the same time. We're still at that point in our household where our children are fascinated by things that Daddy has written.

I also want to tell you here that writing for young people will not affect your writing for other markets. Some of you may be wondering why I'm including this. It's because I'm often told by beginning writers that they think writing for young people will damage their writing for adults. I think they're probably thinking that the simpler language will be difficult to overcome when they're writing their adult stories. A lot of people who start out writing for young people really want to write for young people but also want to expand into the adult market. This is fine. You can do it. There are a lot of similarities, but there are also a lot of differences. In addition to writing for young people, I write adult spy/espionage stories, and I have no problem doing this.

The rewards from writing for young people are many. Writing in itself gives a lot of joy, and I think that's what helps to keep writers writing when they get bogged down in the agony of trying to extract stories from wherever it is that stories come from. Then there is, of course, the financial reward. You should never be afraid to admit that this is one of the reasons you're writing. But the other rewards are nice, too. It's nice when you're in a bookstore and you hear somebody you've never met before asking for one of your collections of short stories. It's nice when you're in a library and you find your name in the card catalog (or in the computer) or see somebody reading one of your stories. It's nice when a teacher in the public school system calls you up and tells you that her students are studying your stories and wants to know if you'd be interested in coming to speak to one of her classes. It's nice when you're asked to speak at writers' conferences on writing short stories for young people. It's especially nice when somebody asks you to write a book about it!

If you've now decided that you have the talent for writing for young people, and if you're willing to study and work hard, then you're already well on your way to becoming a writer. The primary purpose of this book is to help you become a *published* writer. I've arranged the chapters in the order most likely to help you gain the skills needed to achieve this.

2

Why the Short Story?

If you want to become a professional writer as fast as you possibly can, then you should definitely start with short stories. But don't start out with the wrong approach. Even though beginning writers think writing a short story will be easy, they soon find that it takes a lot of time, effort, and just plain hard work to write a good one. But—and this is important—it doesn't take as much time as it does to write a novel!

All categories of short stories are found in magazines for young people, but the basic rules for writing the short story are the same. According to a recent survey, there are almost 400 publications buying short stories for young people. Many of these publications are published once a week, which means that they use a great deal of material, most of it freelance. I'll say more about markets in Chapter Twenty.

As a writer of short stories for young people, you can capture all the things that young people care to read about. Your subject matter is the human experience itself, for today there are really very few taboos, considering the whole range of publications for

11

young people. I honestly believe you can write about anything, as long as you do it with skill, compassion, good taste, and honesty. Somewhere, you'll be able to find an audience.

Young people find the short story the most approachable and the most satisfying of all literary forms. It allows them to discover how things turned out in a relatively short period of time. This can be to the advantage of the beginning writer. You can channel all your artistic efforts into a story that you know will find a readership and into a length you'll find easier to handle in terms of character, setting, and plot.

Some young people choose the short story because of the characters who live within it. They want to know how other young people live and talk and behave in circumstances either similar to or different from their own. For instance, in Frank Carson Knebel's "Tjurunga," the reader follows Jungari on his "journey into manhood" through Australia's Great Victoria Desert, a journey that is interrupted when Jungari witnesses an airplane crash and then has to take care of the survivors. Young people are interested in the individual characters in this story and in their relationships to each other.

Some young people read a short story for what it says. It pleases a young person to no end to read a passage in a story that verbalizes exactly what he has been feeling for so long but just hasn't been able to put into words. These passages represent interpretations of the secrets of life. When I was young, I used to underline certain passages in the short stories I was reading, because they contained my philosophy for living. Since many young people haven't developed their own philosophies or at least not yet put them in writing, they look to passages in what they read to put into words exactly what they've been feeling.

But some young people don't read a short story just for its action, its characters, or its philosophy—they stay with it because of the form itself. We can all remember paying tribute to narration. How many of you remember how, when you were children, you'd correct your parents because they had omitted a favorite passage from your favorite story? Actually, I can't remember doing this myself, but I can certainly remember my own children doing this. (It happened only last night, in fact!) The scene is always the same. It's late. It's way past bedtime. I really don't want to read the story, because I'm tired and cranky and I have a million and one things to do before I go to bed myself, but I feel the need to be the dutiful father and read the requested bedtime story and . . . I start it and find myself thinking, well, I'll skip over this next passage, because it isn't very interesting and they're probably not listening anyway. What happens? You skip over the passage, your child stops you, tells you—no, quotes for you verbatim—the passage you skipped, so you have to go back and read it, adding extra minutes for this omission. What is it that you've actually done? You've destroyed the narrative of the story. The child realizes that a part is missing and that the story isn't complete without that part. Yes, we all realize very early one of the major components of the short story.

I doubt if many young people read a short story for style alone, because we're getting into more sophisticated literary analyses here; but whether consciously or subconsciously, young people do recognize style. They readily recognize their favorite authors, and, in doing so, they recognize style. A young person might be hard pressed to consider such problems as point-of-view and structure, but he definitely responds to the language of the story, to the rhythm, to the images created by the writer, and yes, even to the symbols and the arrangements of words within sentences and sentences within paragraphs.

Young people are drawn to the rhymes and rhythms of stories by Dr. Seuss, as in *The Cat in the Hat:*

"And then
Something went bump!
How that bump made us jump!"

and to the images of Rudyard Kipling, as in one of his *Just So Stories,* "How the Camel Got His Hump":

"And the Camel said 'Humph!' again; but no sooner had he said it than he saw his back, that he was so proud of, puffing up into a great big lolloping humph."

13

WRITING SHORT STORIES FOR YOUNG PEOPLE

How long should you stay with short stories if you're also interested in other forms? Well, at least for a while. Remember, short stories don't take as long to write as novels. That means you might write a large number of short stories in a relatively short period of time. And by continuing to write, you continue to improve. Even though the story you've just sent out is the best one you could have written, the next one, believe me, will be even better. You do get better and better every time you write another story. It's incredible, but this is the way it happens. You see things you didn't see before. If you look at a story you've just written, you may think it couldn't possibly be any better; but once it's published, if you waited a year, continuing to write other stories, then looked at this story again, you'd see many things you'd change. This happens because you're constantly growing as a writer.

By continuing to write and send out your stories, you're also hedging against the possibility of rejection. Somewhere out there is an editor who'll like you and your work, because that's the way the world is. Just as there are editors who'll never like your work, there are editors who'll like everything you write.

If you continue to send out short stories to the same publication, even if you've been rejected several times by that publication, there's still a very positive element to what you're doing. The editors at the publication are getting to know you, and they're able to see you as a writer who can produce. This is very important. Editors of magazines want writers who can produce, prolific writers. It won't be long before you're accepted (and here I'm certainly thinking that your work is acceptable to begin with, but just hasn't hit the mark or been what the editors were really looking for), and it won't be long before the editor calls you on the phone and asks you to write a story for him. Something happens sometimes that just can't be explained. All of a sudden, after all these stories have been rejected, you're suddenly noticed and you're a hot property. An analogy would be any overnight success story, which never is really an *overnight* success story.

It's very exciting when you suddenly become an editor's favorite contributor. I once had several series running in several magazines. I could call the editors up on the telephone and they would talk to me! They would *want* to talk to me! Still, they expected me to have my stories in by their deadlines. They knew I would. I had gained their trust—they knew I wouldn't disappoint them.

If an editor takes an interest in you, then by all means take advantage of it. Try to work with him even on what you may consider impossible deadlines. I have often drastically rearranged my whole schedule to accommodate a magazine's deadline or a particular editor's request to do something. I felt that, as a beginning writer, I had to do so to prove myself. It was important to me that I become known as somebody who could be counted on to produce and to produce on time. If you're saying, "Well, I'm not going to give up this or I'm not going to give up that just to get a short story published in a particular magazine," then you may not really want to become a writer badly enough.

No editor is going to ask anything really impossible of you. What may seem an impossibility may be because what you're asked to do hasn't yet become a part of your schedule. What I'm saying is that, if you're interested in becoming a writer, your daily schedule may have to be altered to achieve this goal. Take advantage of the situation and alter your schedule. This alteration won't last forever. The better known you become, the more freedom you'll have. But you have to get to that point first. You have to build up a track record that'll lead you to bigger and better things.

There was a long period of time in my life when I wrote only one short story a month. Looking back on that period now, I can't honestly tell you why that's all I did, but it was, and I was perfectly satisfied. It filled my need to be a published writer, but the need then probably wasn't as great as it has since become, and I think that's a normal development. I think we develop into writers. I think that for some of us it's absolutely necessary that we take it easy and let ourselves evolve into writers. I used to wonder how in the world some of my writing friends wrote on several different stories and books at the same time. I'd think I'd never be able to do that, but I *was* able, and I *am* able, and you'll be able, too. You'll evolve into it; it really is an evolutionary process that's taking place. It isn't something that you should rush, this process of becoming a writer. Take my word for it.

15

As I developed, I got to the point where I began getting ideas for other stories and other series and other characters. I'd been working long enough with some of my editors that I felt quite comfortable in suggesting these new ideas to them. Some of them were accepted. Some weren't. Some even became the bases for entire magazines. At one time, I had seven series running at the same time (some stayed longer in the magazines than others), but soon the evolutionary process took over and I got to the point where I wanted to write books, too. This brings me to the second reason for choosing short stories as a form for your writing.

Writing short stories can be an excellent start for the beginning writer who aspires to write novels for young people. Any beginning writer needs immediate positive psychological reinforcement and some financial reward, and both can be achieved much earlier and much faster with short stories than with novels. After you've mastered the techniques discussed in this book and are a published writer of short stories, you'll be better equipped to write novels for young people. Many of the techniques of short story writing can be applied to the writing of novels, so that'll be helpful, but even more helpful will be the psychological aspect. The beginning writer of novels *who is a selling writer of short stories* will be more relaxed and less likely to suffer from writer's block. You won't have that nagging fear that you're spending months and months on a project, your novel, from which you'll never realize anything.

One easy way of accomplishing this task is to set aside one of your writing days solely for short stories. If you're publishing your short stories, then you'll really think of yourself as a writer; your friends will think of you as a writer; and you'll probably be making enough money to supply yourself with typing paper (needed for those longer novels), typewriter ribbons, and stamps, and have a few dollars left over to celebrate your successes. Without this reinforcement, you could be caught in a situation that discourages even professional writers, but that is especially damaging to the morale of beginning writers. Success gives confidence, and confidence helps writing.

The bottom line is that the beginning writer of novels for

young people is much better able to produce his novels if he is at the same time writing and selling short stories for young people.

Finally, I'd like to mention that I think it's probably unrealistic at this point for you to think about publishing a collection of your short stories in book form; this is seldom done, even with well-known writers; however, you might want to consider using one of your short stories as the basis for a novel. I'll discuss any problems you might have with the right to do this with a *published* short story in Chapter Twenty, "Markets."

Part Two

Choosing the Right Form for Your Story

3

The Mystery Short Story

Young people love mysteries. One reason is that at a very early age, they find themselves in a world of adult secrets, as they perceive it, which they're trying to unravel.

Another reason is that much of the process of growth, and change, and the actions and reactions of other young people—all of immense importance to any young person—are likewise to them secrets in need of figuring out.

Young people also love having secrets, their own or somebody else's. They feel special if somebody confides a secret in them. They feel privileged. On the other hand, young people like to keep their own secrets, because there are things that they don't want other people to know about them. These secrets can range from the very silly to the very serious. The bottom line is that we all like to feel that we can control what other people know about us, and in that way, control what other people think about us.

This, then, is the main reason mysteries appeal so much to young people: mysteries are about secrets.

But it's important to know that secrets aren't always successfully kept. In fact, mystery stories involve one person's trying to find out another person's secrets.

Mysteries for young people may be divided into two distinct types: the *puzzle* story, usually for young readers; and the *crime* story, usually for older readers.

The pure puzzle story has dropped all of its frightening aspects and is merely a puzzle to be figured out. Where did the robin get those bright golden threads for its nest, for instance, or how did the leopard get its spots? These types of stories don't frighten younger people, and they encourage them to use their own powers of deduction along with the main characters.

The crime story, on the other hand, can range from the main character's having to contend with other young people stirring up trouble to the serious crimes of robbery and murder.

From now on, I'll refer to *individual stories* in this category as either "puzzle" stories or "crime" stories. The terms "mystery" and "mystery story" will be used in a general sense.

The crime story is about *who* committed the crime and *why;* it is psychological at its base and often has an *analysis* of why a person committed a certain crime.

Often, however, in crime stories for young people, the interest is not so much in who committed the crime and why, but in the person who's trying to solve the crime. These are generally the characters that the young people get involved with. Nancy Drew, the Dana Girls, the Hardy Boys—all these characters are still solving crimes, and they've been doing so for many years. No matter how you may feel about these characters (and they've certainly prompted a lot of debate), they're still characters that young people like to get involved with. Young people *care* about them.

Young people who read crime stories seem to have a sense for what does and doesn't belong in a story in the way of clues. They'll notice things that aren't right in the story, because at the same time they're reading the story, they're helping the main character solve the crime. That's why it's very important that clues be placed honestly in the crime story you're writing. Young people who read crime stories seem to be the most observant of all readers. They pay very close attention to the clues that the writer has placed in the story, and it gives them a particular thrill if they're able to discover these clues ahead of the main character (not too far ahead, mind you, since in doing that, their attitude toward the main character would change from one of admiration to one of disdain).

At some point in every crime story for young people, the young crime-solver is called upon to risk his life, although it's usually important (except in the young adult stories) that the risk be only in the mind of the main character. There are still editors and parents who frown upon the idea of a main character's seriously risking his life in order to solve a crime, because he's often seen as a role model. Nancy Drew often risked her life, but because she was a series character, there was always the feeling that nothing serious would ever happen to her and that in the end everything would turn out all right. This is one of the safety valves available to series characters that's not often available to one-story characters. Your young crime-solver's judgment must be so good that he may safely take physical risks that will in turn lead to the capture of a criminal and to the solving of the crime.

Young people are especially impressed by survival in the crime story (and even more so in the suspense/adventure story, which I'll discuss in the next chapter), because survival is survival by one's own wits. Usually, the young crime-solver noses around too much for his own good, because he's curious, and is the first to sense that something's wrong somewhere. Your young readers will see this not only as a strength, but as a curse. The young crime-solver simply can't resist a good mystery. In fact, many crime stories for young people start out with similar comments, coming from either the parents or friends, that, "Ah ha! Here's a mystery that so-and-so won't be able to leave alone!" What always saves the young crime-solver is his very clever mind (usually much more clever than the average character's or reader's mind!), his intuition, and his ability to make sense out of all the clues that are supposed to seem unimportant to the other characters in the story and to the reader. In the actual writing of the story, the clues should be the most obvious to the main character, the next most obvious to the reader, and the least obvious to the other characters in the story. A writer certainly doesn't want the reader to be smarter than the young crime-solver, but he wants him to be smarter than the other characters. This allows a bond to develop between the reader and the main character. This gives the reader a sense of accomplishment without making him so smart that he thinks the young crime-solver is a dope! He has to have admiration for the main character or he won't want to finish the story. But he should also feel a certain camaraderie with the main character that'll lead him to think that if he were in the story he'd actually be a closer friend than some of the fictional friends.

Young people like to think they can outsmart other people by their wit and their wisdom. They particularly enjoy saying, "I knew he'd do that!" or "I told you so!"

How do you write a crime story? Well, first of all, there must be a crime. The crime may be committed against a person, against an object, or against a place. If the crime is committed against a person, it can involve a schoolyard bully who shoves, pinches, or in general irritates people; a murderer; or any type of offender in between. If the crime is against a thing, it can range from somebody stealing somebody's school lunch or books or whatever, to the most serious crime (in the way of social punishment) of stealing automobiles. If the crime is committed against a place, it can range from making marks on the walls of a building to the serious vandalization of that same building.

Next, the crime must be discovered. If the crime isn't discovered, then you have no story. Who discovers the crime? Often, it can be the young crime-solver. Or it can be somebody who's heard how successful the young crime-solver is at solving crimes and who's now contacting him for help.

After the crime has been discovered, the young crime-solver comes into the story. He usually has to have a reason for solving the crime. Of course, it can be that he simply likes to solve crimes, thereby helping humanity. But chances are it would be better for you and for your story if he's solving the crime for a special reason. He could be helping a friend or the friend of a friend. He could be helping his parents or his brothers and sisters. It gives him a much more acceptable reason if he has a valid, personal connection to the crime. Of course, if the crime story is to be taken seriously, and therefore to be entertaining, something must depend on the crime's being solved. Some evil must be avoided or be defeated, and some good must usually be achieved.

The next thing the young crime-solver does is to try to find out if anybody else knows anything at all about the crime. He'll try to ferret out as much information as possible from the person against whom the crime has been committed or from people who'll suffer the most from the crime. It would be quite unusual in a story (and usually wouldn't work) to have a witness who's seen the crime committed and knows the identity of the criminal. Usually, there will be several people who provide bits and pieces of *how* the crime could have been committed; this information allows your young crime-solver to put the puzzle together and solve the crime.

What the young crime-solver does next is to question the suspects (or in some cases, simply to observe the suspects). Some suspects should seem more guilty than others. The reader might mistakenly select one of these suspects as having actually committed the crime. But your young crime-solver will know all along that that suspect couldn't have committed the crime, and he'll tell the reader why at the end of the story. What the young crime-solver will need to determine is which one of the suspects had the *motive* for committing the crime. It'll be up to the young crime-solver to put the motive and the suspect together.

It's usually in the motive that any psychological information is given to the reader. Young crime-solvers, however, don't often go too far into determining all the psychological reasons that a crime has been committed. A young person might steal a pencil, for example, because his parents either didn't have the money to give him to buy it or wouldn't for some other reason give him the money. For adults, it's usually not enough to know how a crime was committed and who committed it; adults also want to know *why* the crime was committed. Some young people are also interested—up to a point—in why a person committed a crime. When they finish a crime story, they'll often want to know "why the criminal did that." The writer of crime short stories for young people can often explain the motive of a crime in a few sentences without getting into textbook psychological reasons. The higher up the reading level a writer writes for, however, the more he's able to delve into these psychological reasons. Even so, I think writers are often surprised to learn just how early young people are interested in why a person committed a crime. Young people discover quite early that they do things they just can't explain. I've unfortunately been guilty, as I'm sure many parents have, of saying to my children, "Why in the world did you do that?" The answer quite often is, "I don't know!" What you have to remember as a writer (and as a parent) is that young people are usually telling you the truth when they say they don't know why they did something and that they'd be interested in reading a possible explanation for behavior, even criminal behavior. Their actions often puzzle them as much as they puzzle their parents.

Motives in the crime story are often revenge, jealousy, greed, fear of having a past action revealed, or an abnormality of some kind. Often in mysteries, young people discover a little of their secret self.

In a crime story, the person who's committed the crime never succeeds entirely in covering up the fact that he's the guilty party. There are enough clues that the young crime-solver can find them and put them all together. The clues that the young crime-solver finds may be things that belong to the criminal or things that are in some way associated with him. These things may be pieces of clothing. They may be other personal belongings. Other clues as to the identification of the criminal may be gathered from other suspects or witnesses.

The young crime-solver follows the suspects and is almost always followed himself. There's usually a chase of some sort in almost every crime story for young people. This gives the story excitement and adventure.

The crime story usually ends with the criminal's confession. The criminal usually makes his confession voluntarily, after he's been confronted with the evidence or at the point of a gun *held by an adult* who's been called in by the young crime-solver. Through this confession, the reader learns the true story of what happened, as put together by the young crime-solver and supplemented by the criminal's confession. All loose ends are tied up at this time.

Although mysteries for young people are usually thought of as something that'll make the reader's hair stand on end, they don't have to be such. Mysteries for young people can also succeed if they're primarily intellectual. By that, I mean that they can appeal to young people's enjoyment of solving puzzles, that is, coming up with the right answer, preferably before anybody else! Young people have an interest in puzzle solving from the very early stages of their reading.

Once in a while, a mystery will provide the writer a chance to teach a "lesson of life" to a young person, but the primary reason that young people read mysteries is for escape.

Consider, then, what happens in a crime story for young people:

1. A crime is committed.

2. The crime is discovered.

3. The young crime-solver comes up with several suspects.

4. More crimes are committed, as the criminal tries to keep his identity from the young crime-solver.

5. The young crime-solver begins to get close to the truth and finally puts it all together.

6. The criminal is confronted and confesses.

Action, which is more important in the suspense/adventure story, as you'll see in the next chapter, is usually confined in a crime story to the young crime-solver's trying to find out who committed the crime. Generally, any action in the crime story comes at the end when there's often a chase scene, as the young crime-solver discovers who the criminal is.

Background is important in the crime story, because it needs to be realistic enough for the reader to believe that the story could actually take place there. Once you've decided on the background for your crime story, usually a couple of sentences at the beginning will be sufficient to make your reader feel that he is indeed where you say he is.

It's the area of character motivation that you have to pay particular attention to in the crime story. You must remember that all the characters in a crime story are basically pieces of a puzzle and that the reader will be trying to fit them all together to discover just what part of the puzzle fits where. If your characters' motivations are weak, then your readers won't want to read about your characters, and if your reader doesn't want to read about your characters, you're in serious trouble! The criminal has to have a motive for committing the crime. Similarly, the young crime-solver has to have a motive for solving the crime. Different people in the story have to have motives for either giving or withholding information from the young crime-solver. If you're interested in writing mysteries for young people, then you'd do well to work out all your characters' motivations before you begin writing your story.

I'd now like for you to read a mystery story of mine which is a crime story *with a puzzle;* then I'll analyze it.

The Alphabet Letter Mystery

BY GEORGE STANLEY

Eva Lopez de Perez stepped off the Pullman car at the railway station in Ojinaga. The trip from Chihuahua City had been much more pleasant than she would have imagined. A porter helped her with her suitcase, and she gave him a few *centavos.* She promised him that there would be several *pesos* if he could get her a taxi right away to take her across the bridge to Presidio, Texas.

A taxi appeared almost instantly, and Eva Lopez de Perez gave the porter the several *pesos* she had promised.

"Where to?" the taxi driver asked.

"The Victoria Hotel, Presidio," she replied.

"You'll need some sort of identification when we cross the river, senora."

"I know," Eva said pleasantly. "I have my Mexican passport."

She gave her passport to the driver and settled into the backseat of the taxi for the short drive. Her passport was in order. *No worry.* She had nothing but a few clothes in her suitcase. *No worry.* In her handbag she had no marijuana or heroin or whatever the American authorities were always looking for. *No worry.* So it took her no time at all to cross the border. To the American authorities she was just a respectable Mexican woman coming to the United States. They just assumed that after spending the night in Presidio she would be going on to Dallas to shop or to San Antonio to visit friends. This was exactly the impression she wanted to convey, for respectable Eva Lopez de

Perez was actually KGB agent Nina Polpova, in charge of Soviet activities in northern Mexico.

Once across the bridge, Nina Polpova opened her handbag and took out a postcard with a picture of the Victoria Hotel in Presidio on it. On the back was a message.

"Father is very ill. Come . . ." was all she read before her head went through the windshield of the taxi, severing her throat, and draining every bit of life from her body.

* * *

Police Chief Andy Henderson was watching the ambulance attendants cover the body of the woman when a reporter from the Presidio newspaper approached.

"What happened?" the reporter asked as he arrived at the scene of the accident.

"Some wetback hit 'em," Henderson said. "Stole a car to try and make it up north. Didn't even know how to drive. Woman's dead, and the taxi driver's cut up pretty bad. Probably won't make it."

"Who's the woman?" the reporter asked.

"Mexican, don't know her name yet," Henderson replied. "But she just crossed the border. Probably got off the train from Chihuahua City."

The reporter made his way through the crowd to peek under the sheet that covered the dead woman. Henderson was just about to get into the patrol car when he saw his deputy approaching.

"Here's her handbag," Deputy Suarez said. "Most of the contents were on the floor of the taxi. Passport, lipstick, powder, and so forth. She must have had the bag open, unless the impact . . ."

"Probably powdering her nose or putting on her lipstick. Just like a woman."

"This was on the floorboard, too," the deputy said, handing Henderson a postcard. "It's a picture of the Victoria Hotel here in town. It was mailed from here a couple of weeks ago."

Henderson looked at the card. It was addressed to a senora Eva Lopez de Perez, Calle Orito, Chihuahua City. The message was short and in English: "Father is very ill. Come at once." It was signed " Ж "

"If her father is very ill," Suarez said, "this will probably kill him."

But Henderson wasn't paying any attention. He was looking at the signature.

"What's this look like to you?" he asked the deputy.

"An *X*?" the deputy asked after a moment.

"Mighty peculiar-looking *X,* isn't it?"

"Maybe it's a couple of letters together, like *X* and *I,*" Suarez said, "or a brand or something. Anyway, what difference does it make?"

"Just seems so unlike the rest of the message," Henderson replied. "It's like another language. And why is the message written in English instead of Spanish?"

"Well, I . . ." Suarez began.

Henderson interrupted, "Doesn't it seem strange to you that someone would *write* a daughter about her father's illness instead of *telephoning* her? Look how long it took from the time they mailed the postcard until the time she got here today. And why send the message on a postcard from the Victoria Hotel?"

"Well, I . . ." was all Deputy Suarez had time to say again before Henderson started getting into the patrol car, his mind now on what he still had to do. He needed to notify whomever it was that Eva Lopez de Perez was coming to visit. If she really was coming to visit a sick father, then he'd have to check with every Lopez in town until he found the right one. Since she had had no local identification on her, that could take several hours.

He drove with the deputy back to the office and deposited the woman's things with the desk sergeant. He gave the sergeant the woman's Chihuahua address and told him to try to contact the Chihuahua authorities. Maybe he'd be lucky. Then Henderson and Suarez began telephoning all of the Lopezes listed in the Presidio telephone directory.

After they had telephoned the home of the twentieth Lopez, to no avail, Deputy Suarez said, "Can you imagine what a job this would be if this were Mexico City?"

"If this were Mexico City," Henderson replied, "there'd probably be an easier way of doing this."

Two hours later, Henderson and Suarez telephoned the last Lopez listed in the Presidio telephone directory.

"Maybe that's why they wrote instead of telephoning," Suarez said. "Maybe they're too poor to have a telephone."

"Could be," Henderson said. "We may have to have someone check the city directory or the welfare rolls or . . . wait a minute, suppose she could have been going to the Victoria Hotel instead of to her father's house."

"But why?" Suarez asked.

"Well, if her parents really are poor, maybe there just wasn't any room for her at home," Henderson replied. "Anyway, it certainly won't hurt to go to the Victoria Hotel and talk to the desk clerk. We don't have much else to go on."

All the desk clerk could do was to confirm that the hotel had indeed received a telephone call from a senora Lopez de Perez the first of the week, wanting a room for one night. But he didn't know anything about the woman's sick father. Nor could he remember any particular person's mailing a postcard from the hotel, since several were usually sent every day.

"If she had family in Presidio, why didn't someone meet her at the train?" Henderson asked, as he and Suarez left the hotel. "And why just stay one night if her father were sick?"

"None of this makes much sense to me," Suarez said.

"You know," Henderson said, as he and Suarez got into the patrol car, "I think it's all tied up with that signature, or whatever it is."

"You mean it might be a secret code?" Suarez asked, remembering Henderson's taste for spy novels.

"Well," Henderson replied, "it doesn't look like any alphabet letter I've ever seen."

The next morning, Henderson placed a telephone call to the foreign language department at Rio Grande University.

"Let me speak to the person in charge," he said.

"That would be Professor Meyers," the girl on the line said politely.

"Professor Meyers here," a soft voice said, after a moment.

"Professor, this is Police Chief Henderson in Presidio. I have a problem down here. I was wondering if you could help me with it."

"I shall try," the professor said very precisely.

"I'm driving up to the county seat today," Henderson continued, "and I was wondering if I could come by and talk to you."

"Certainly," Professor Meyers said. "I shall be in my office all afternoon."

Henderson found Professor Meyers in a small, stuffy office behind the Administration Building. He was almost hidden by several stacks of books.

"Sorry to disturb you, Professor," Henderson said.

"That's quite all right," Meyers said, motioning Henderson to a dusty chair. "Now, what may I do for you?"

31

Henderson handed the professor the postcard.

"It's the signature that puzzles me," he said. "It doesn't look at all like English."

Meyers put on his glasses and looked at the symbol on the postcard.

"Quite right," he said, "it's Cyrillic."

"Cy . . . what?" Henderson asked.

"Cyrillic," Meyers repeated, "an alphabet attributed to St. Cyril, the ninth-century Greek prelate who was an apostle to the Slavs. It's based on the Greek alphabet. Several Slavic languages are written in the alphabet. English uses the Latin alphabet, of course."

"Well, of course . . ." Henderson finally said, not wanting to appear too ignorant.

"Russian is written in the Cyrillic alphabet," Professor Meyers continued, "as is Bulgarian . . ."

"Russian!" Henderson said.

"Yes, it is," Meyers said.

"Well, what does that symbol mean?" Henderson asked.

"It doesn't actually mean anything," Meyers replied. "It's just a letter. It's usually pronounced like *zheh* or *zhe,* but neither pronunciation really means anything. It would be the same as saying *s* or *z* or some other letter, that's all."

"You don't know why someone would use that symbol on a postcard as a signature, do you?" Henderson asked.

"No," Meyers replied, "not unless it's the first letter of someone's name, but I'm just not that familiar with Russian patronymics, so it would be quite a chore to figure out just what name."

Henderson had decided halfway through Professor Meyers's explanation that he was getting absolutely nowhere, so he didn't even bother to ask what patronymics meant. Although the mysterious senora Eva Lopez de Perez was still mysterious, Henderson had begun to feel that he was making entirely too much out of a symbol on an ordinary postcard.

Henderson thanked Professor Meyers for his help and left the stuffy little book-filled room. *I would never have fit into this type of world,* he thought as he left the campus.

He drove straight to his rooming house and called his office to tell them that he was back and didn't want to be disturbed unless it was absolutely necessary.

His trip to the county seat and to the professor's stuffy office had left him with a bad taste in his mouth. He'd been ridiculous to think there was anything sinister about the signature on the postcard. He'd have to quit reading so many novels about beautiful young spies on trains and secret coded messages. There had to be a reasonable explanation of the lady's identity. He'd probably hear from Chihuahua in a few days and the whole matter would be settled.

Henderson took the supper his landlady, Mrs. Garza, had cooked for him to his room, opened a can of cola, turned on the television, and lay down on the bed.

The telephone awakened him at 11:15. He lifted the receiver on the third shattering ring.

"Henderson," he said sleepily.

"Chief Henderson?" a soft voice said," this is Professor Meyers. I hope I'm not disturbing you."

"Oh, no, not at all," Henderson said, wondering what Meyers could possibly want with him at this hour.

"You know that postcard you showed me today, the one with the Cyrillic symbol?"

"Yes," Henderson replied.

"Well, something just dawned on me," Meyers said, "something almost silly, really."

Come on, man, Henderson thought, *get to the point.* "Yes," he said, again.

"Well, as I said, it's not a word as such, just a letter. But I suddenly remembered that there *is* one place where you will see it by itself and where it *does* have a meaning. In fact, if you're a woman, it has a very important meaning."

"Yes, yes!" Henderson thought his last "yes" a bit testy, but the professor didn't seem to notice.

"It means rest room," Meyers continued, "that is, a women's rest room."

"What?" Henderson shouted, sitting up. "Rest room?"

"Yes," Meyers said, quite thrilled with this revelation, "rest room. In America we have the words *ladies* or *women* on rest-room doors, the Russians would have the symbol 'Ж' . It stands for *zhehnshcheeni,* 'Ж' being the first . . ."

"Well, that's very good news, Professor Meyers," Henderson said as politely as he could. "I'll remember that. Thank you for calling."

"Think nothing of it. Good-night," Professor Meyers said.

"Good-night," Henderson said, and hung up the receiver.

Chief Henderson thought about Professor Meyers's revelations: *Rest room! Of all the nonsense! Victoria Hotel. Rest room. It would really be too much like . . .*

In a few minutes, he was parked in front of the Victoria Hotel. He knew Sam, the night desk clerk.

"Sam," he said, as he entered the lobby, "I'm going to use the ladies' rest room."

"That's what you think, Henderson," Sam said.

But Henderson proceeded to the end of the lobby, opened the door to the ladies' rest room, shouted, "Anybody in there?" and, not getting an answer, went in.

It didn't take him long to find what he wanted. Taped underneath the water tank in the last stall was a small metal container the size of a dime. Henderson put the container in his pocket and left the ladies' room.

"Thanks, Sam," he shouted, "I feel much better."

"You're just plain weird, Henderson," Sam said, not showing his face from behind a yellowed copy of a magazine.

Back in his room, Henderson studied the small container under a light. He could see small slits where it could be opened. Getting a pair of tweezers from the bathroom, he pried the container's lid off. Inside were several loose black dots. They looked very much to Henderson like the same type of material as film negatives.

Henderson smiled. He thought of telephoning Professor Meyers, but decided he'd telephone the El Paso office of the FBI first.

Several questions must be answered before you can call your story a crime story:

1. Does your story open with a crime having been committed in the first few paragraphs? If it doesn't, it should. You shouldn't spend a lot of time working up to the crime. The crime is the reason for the story in the first place, and the reason your reader is reading the story is to solve the crime. He wants to start right away.

In the first nine paragraphs (including dialogue) of "The Alphabet Letter Mystery," the crime is committed. The reader learns that Eva Lopez de Perez, who's crossed the Mexican border into Presidio, Texas, is actually KGB agent Nina Polpova, in charge of Soviet activities in northern Mexico. At least one crime that the reader is aware of is that the person has crossed the border under an assumed name. A mystery is also hinted at in the post card. It seems to contain a mysterious message. The crime, as the reader either suspects or learns later, is that of entering the United States to commit espionage. I'd also like to add here that the death of this agent is rather violent, but it was still accepted by the editor because it fit the story. Nina Polpova was in an automobile accident, "severing her throat and draining every bit of life from her body." I felt a violent death was necessary to the story. It would attract immediate police attention—more, perhaps, than a less violent one.

2. Does your young crime-solver appear near the beginning of the story? If he doesn't, he should. Some crime stories will use the first-person viewpoint, and with this technique, the young crime-solver could be the person who discovers the crime. Or if you have a bias against first-person point-of-view, then you can begin with somebody telling the young crime-solver about a crime that has just been committed. But the crime and the young crime-solver need to appear as soon as the story starts. (Point-of-view will be discussed in Chapter Nine.)

In "The Alphabet Letter Mystery," the young crime-solver appears immediately after the crime has been committed. He's the

Police Chief of Presidio, Texas, and he's the one who'll be investigating the crime. Here, a rule in writing stories for young people has been bent somewhat. The main character is a few years older (but not many) than is usual for the age range of the story. Chief Andy Henderson is, however, a *younger* police chief, probably in his early- to mid-twenties (not at all unusual in small Texas towns), more modern than most, and so he is acceptable. His occupation is among those that interest young people. If he had been an architect, then he probably wouldn't have been accepted as readily.

It's generally better to avoid adult protagonists in stories for young people, however, because such protagonists limit your market; but if your story calls for an older protagonist, as "The Alphabet Letter Mystery" did, then use one.

3. Does the young crime-solver have a good reason for wanting to solve the case?   He must. He could be helping a friend, a teacher, or his parents, but he must have a more significant reason than simply liking to solve mysteries. Young readers won't readily accept it otherwise.

In "The Alphabet Letter Mystery," this problem was easily solved. The main character, the young crime-solver, is the chief-of-police. He has a very good reason for getting involved in solving the crime that has taken place in his city. It's his job. He's paid to solve crimes.

4. Is the crime that's been committed of sufficient interest to your reader? Is it too violent or not violent enough?   The amount of violence you use in your crime story should be determined by the age group. This will usually range from no violence at all in preschool stories to adult-level violence in young-adult stories. My advice is to write your story and include in it any violence you feel is necessary and then let your editor decide whether or not it should stay.

Editors of publications that accept violence in stories realize that there are some young people who aren't interested in reading about crimes unless they're serious crimes, the kind one finds on the front page of a newspaper. Some publications, however, won't accept mysteries with violent crimes at any age level. Those that won't usually say so in their writer's guidelines. You must pay attention to these guidelines, because they mean what they say.

There is, as you have already seen, a violent death in "The Alphabet Letter Mystery," and it wasn't cut by the editor. As for the crime of espionage, I think the following elements of it in the story will interest the reader: (a) the setting of the crime; (b) the unusual signature on the post card, which seems to be in code; and (c) the puzzle surrounding the identity of the woman who was killed.

5. Do you introduce at least one suspect in the first few paragraphs of your story? And do you introduce enough suspects throughout your story to keep your reader confused as to who actually committed the crime? You should make sure that there's at least one suspect in the beginning of your story, and you should have enough possible suspects in your story that your reader won't be able to solve the mystery right away.

The first suspect in "The Alphabet Letter Mystery" is killed immediately, but there's still the mystery surrounding who the suspect actually was. A second suspect in the mystery is the father who's mentioned on the post card. This suspect, however, is never found, because there never actually was a father. In the middle of the story, then, the young crime-solver switches from concentrating on *suspects* to concentrating on *clues* in order to solve the mystery. This, as you can see, is one of the major differences between a *crime mystery* and a *puzzle mystery*. In a crime mystery, an actual person has committed a crime and the mystery becomes a "*who*dunit?" In a puzzle mystery, the *who* is either known or isn't important, and the puzzle is the most important thing to be solved. The job of Police Chief Andy Henderson in this story is to solve the puzzle surrounding the woman who was killed.

6. Do you introduce the remaining suspects in the order that they would normally appear in real life? This is very important. If your story has suspects and your reader is trying

37

to determine which one of the suspects committed the crime, then these suspects should be presented in the order that they would appear in real life. If, for instance, the young crime-solver is investigating a crime committed against a friend and the criminal is actually a member of the family, then that family member would be one of the early suspects, because a crime-solver always starts with those closest to the victim and works outward. He wouldn't start with family friends and acquaintances, then go back to the family members. You then wouldn't be able to bring in the family member who committed the crime at the end of your story in order to keep your reader from guessing who the criminal actually is. You would be cheating your reader.

In "The Alphabet Letter Mystery," the suspects are presented in order. First, there's the woman who crosses the border, and second, there's the father, who's mentioned, but never located, because he doesn't exist. But even in a story in which the suspects turn out to be less important than the clues, the former should be presented in real-life order.

7. Have you provided legitimate clues to the puzzle throughout the story? You must be honest with your reader. I can't stress this enough. Adults may forgive a writer who's not been totally honest, one who slips in a clue so that his crime-solver may solve the crime, but young people will feel absolutely cheated by you if you don't provide legitimate clues for them to try to solve the mystery in your story. You must present these clues in the order that the young crime-solver would find them. You mustn't hold back important clues from your reader just because you think they'll give away your story. Remember, your clues should be worked into your story so well that your reader will actually miss them the first time through and will only say, "Oh, sure!" after he has finished the story and sees that he missed the most important clues—clues that you honestly provided but hid so well that they weren't recognized. This is the secret to a successful mystery.

In "The Alphabet Letter Mystery," the clues are provided in order:

38

a. The first clue is the picture of the Victoria Hotel on the post card.

b. The second clue is the message on the post card.

c. The third clue is the peculiar signature on the post card.

d. The fourth clue is the interpretation of the symbol/ signature on the post card.

All of these clues are examined by the chief-of-police and his deputy, who suggest possible solutions to the puzzle. Their solutions, however, purposely lead the reader astray, until finally, the chief-of-police puts everything together and finds the micro dot.

8. Does the tension in the story come from the reader's desire to know a) who committed the crime or b) what the puzzle is concerning the crime? It's important that the tension come from one of these elements. If the story is a crime mystery, then *who* committed the crime will be important to your reader. If you're writing a puzzle mystery, then the solution to the puzzle will be the most important thing to your reader.

In "The Alphabet Letter Mystery," the most important thing to the reader is the solution to the puzzle, since the reader already knows who committed the crime.

9. Do your clues want to make the reader continue reading the story? They should. If the reader thinks he's on his way to solving the mystery, then he's likely to continue reading the story. If he's totally frustrated, because you've either provided insufficient clues or hidden them too well, he won't want to continue reading. There should always be some clues that seem obvious. These, however, can be red herrings. Try to have each clue evoke more and more anticipation in your reader. Make him want to keep reading because he thinks he's solving the mystery.

10. Does the main character seem to be investigating the clues thoroughly, exhausting every avenue but

meeting dead ends everywhere, until it seems that he'll be unable to determine either a) who committed the crime or b) what the solution to the puzzle is? Every time your crime-solver finds a clue and investigates it, he should *seem* to meet a dead end. He should become frustrated, but just a little less frustrated than your reader in wondering who· committed the crime or what the solution to the puzzle is. Remember, this frustration stems from having the clues and simply not being able to put them together. (This is a different type of frustration from the frustration mentioned in item 9.) Your crime-solver should seem so stumped that everything he encounters will make the reader think that the criminal will get away with the crime or that the puzzle won't be solved. But just at the point when the main character seems to have reached a dead end, another clue should surface that will move the story forward.

In "The Alphabet Letter Mystery," Police Chief Andy Henderson thinks he's reached several dead ends, only to have another clue appear that moves the investigation forward, until he feels he's reached another dead end, when the appearance of still another clue moves the story forward again. This continues until finally the police chief is able to put everything together and solve the puzzle.

11. If you use police/detective procedures in your story, are your descriptions accurate? They have to be! Young people today are more knowledgeable about police procedures than you might think. They've seen enough police shows on television to be able to discern whether or not you know what you're talking about. Police departments often give talks in schools and have exhibits of how police conduct their investigations. Your accounts of police procedures, therefore, need to ring true.

In "The Alphabet Letter Mystery," the police procedures are typical of the police procedures in a smaller town, even a border town, where international incidents such as that depicted could occur.

12. Does the solution to the crime come about because the crime-solver has had the main clue all along but simply hadn't put it together properly with the other clues? It should. And this is extremely important. You can't simply throw in a clue at the last moment and expect the reader to accept it as the solution to the crime or the puzzle. Young people, especially, will feel cheated, because solving the mystery is very important to them. You must be fair with your reader. And in any case, your editor probably wouldn't let you get away with it.

In "The Alphabet Letter Mystery," Chief Henderson has had the solution to the puzzle from the beginning. It was simply a matter of putting it all together, and in this case, with the help of the linguistics professor, understanding the exact meaning of the Russian symbol.

13. Does the solution to the crime/puzzle come toward the end of the story? It should. If you solve your crime or puzzle too early in the story, your reader will stop reading. If you still have several paragraphs of information that you want to give your readers, then you'll probably be out of luck, because chances are it won't be read.

In "The Alphabet Letter Mystery," the solution to the puzzle is found in the last two paragraphs of the story. In other words, the reader has to read to the end of the story in order to find out the solution.

Along with everything else I've mentioned, a mystery story must be mysterious. Something must happen in the story that can't be easily explained. The story must be such that the main characters set off to track down the solution, no matter what the obstacles.

Because the writer of a mystery short story must deposit clues along the way for the main characters to discover, a mystery story must be charted *along the way*. It's very difficult to write a mystery story by simply plunging in and seeing what you'll come up with.

It's also a very good idea to read some of the current mystery stories for young people to see what's being bought.

41

There's a definite difference between juvenile mysteries and adult mysteries, and there's a definite difference between mysteries for preschoolers and mysteries for young adults. There was a time not long ago when an editor wouldn't think of buying a short story with a dead body in it (and some still won't!) or a life-threatening situation for the young crime-solver. Thank goodness we're moving away from that.

Your public library almost always has a good selection of young people's magazines that accept mystery stories. Look for *Jack and Jill, Child Life,* or *Boys' Life,* among others. Or if you want your own copies, check *Writer's Market* or *Fiction Writer's Market* for the publishers' addresses. They'll be glad to send you a sample copy, usually for return postage and a small fee.

Editors are deciding that young people can enter into the spirit of a good mystery, even one with an unsavory crime, and not feel the need to rush out and commit the same crime themselves. What they've finally realized is that mysteries aren't blueprints for what young people will do, but simply an escape into a world that they probably would never enter—or even want to enter—in real life.

4

The Suspense/ Adventure Short Story

In this chapter, I've combined two categories, the suspense story and the adventure story. They are, in fact, hard to separate.

A true suspense story has suspense, certainly—or tension, if you prefer—throughout. It's usually the reader's awareness of an impending disaster that creates the tension. A true suspense story doesn't necessarily have an adventure, at least to the extent of a pure adventure story. There may be a chase scene near the end, but the adventure then is just a component of the suspense story.

An example of a true suspense story would be that of a young girl in a house alone who begins to receive frightening telephone calls. The whole story could take place in the house and in the mind of the young girl. She could hear noises, as the terror mounts, but if nobody gets into the house and her parents finally arrive home, then this would be purely a suspense story. If, however, toward the end of the story, somebody breaks into the house and the girl has to run from room to room or from house to house escaping from this person, then we've added the extra element of adventure to the story.

The adventure story, on the other hand, can have elements of suspense, but in the true adventure, the suspense doesn't usually stay at such a high level of tension throughout as it does in a suspense story.

An example of a pure adventure story would be that of a young man or young woman paddling a canoe through a virgin forest. It could be an exciting adventure, because it's something that the young man or young woman has always wanted to do, but if we add no suspense, then it's purely an adventure story (and frankly might get just a little dull after a while). If, however, we add raging rapids, some unscrupulous hunters who try to do the young man or young woman in, some wild animals who attack the protagonist at night, then we've added suspense to the story and we have a suspense/adventure story.

Most short stories for young people in these categories combine *both* the elements of suspense and adventure; for this reason, I'm combining them for discussion.

In a suspense/adventure story, a young person can test his wits and strength against an awesome opponent. This opponent may be nature. It may be a human being. But if the antagonist is an alien, a witch, or someone with superhuman powers, the story would be fantasy or science fiction, not straight suspense/adventure. The opponents may have great advantages of strength and experience as compared to the hero, but all the people and action should stay within the bounds of what could really happen in the everyday world. That young readers know the dangers are really possible is part of the excitement of this kind of story.

The hero of a suspense/adventure story is motivated by a need to attain a certain goal. This goal may be a person he's trying to rescue from some awful fate. It may be a place he wants to reach—the top of a mountain or the bottom of the ocean. It may be something he wants to possess, such as priceless jewels, valuable coins, precious metals, secret weapons, or secret formulae.

In a suspense/adventure story, the main character moves toward his goal while the opposing forces (the opponent) place all sorts of obstacles in his path to keep him from reaching it. These obstacles can be all kinds of things, from criminals, to rock slides, floods, snowstorms, tornadoes, sensitive alarm systems—any sort of believable obstacle you can invent. If it's something that could stop your young adventurer from accomplishing his task, that is, reaching his goal, then you may use it to try and stop him.

In a suspense/adventure story, the main character should never be paralyzed by fear; but, if he's to be a realistic character, he should admit some fear of the opposition. After all, overcoming tremendous odds to reach a goal is what will make the main character heroic. He must be able to say—or at least indicate to the enemy—that he knows that they're bigger than he is, but that with right on his side, he'll win in the end. This is what makes him the hero.

The hero of a young person's suspense/adventure story is realistic, usually, although he may be infected with some idealism, as young people often are. He's courageous, but he's usually not foolish. Young readers are interested in him because he has a purpose. The reader usually respects him because he's put his life or his reputation on the line for this purpose, which can be an ideal, a principle, or a person. You'll usually find that the main characters of mystery and suspense/adventure stories are the most idealistic characters in category fiction. The reason for this is that they're looking for the truth. The young crime-solver tries to find out who committed the crime, while the young adventurer is trying to reach his goal without being compromised.

The young adventurer should be strong and resourceful. He should know himself well enough (or at least discover more about himself in the process of the suspense/adventure) to overcome the evil forces opposing him.

If he's lost in a forest, he can survive by making a bed of pine needles, finding fruit to eat, and making a fire by using either a stick or flint rocks. He's physically strong enough to stand up to the physical stress under which he finds himself. He's not a super hero, but he is indeed a hero. Although nothing he does shows superhuman strength, he's a little more perfect than most of us—not in an obnoxious way, but in a way to be admired, a way to be emulated.

One of the best examples of this type of character is Mark Twain's Huckleberry Finn, with his combination of shrewdness and naivete.

Besides this physical prowess, the young adventurer shows mental prowess. He's smarter than his opponents. He can usually outguess and outthink them. Every obstacle they put in his way he's able to avoid, because he knows enough to outsmart them.

The main themes of almost any suspense/adventure story are superiority and domination. All you have to do is read a suspense/adventure story and you'll readily see this. Thieves may have stolen some precious mementos from the little old lady down the street, but the neighborhood kids aren't going to let them get away with it. They immediately start their search for the thieves. The kids will prove that they're superior to the thieves in that they'll be able to find them, outsmart them, and retrieve the little old lady's valuable possessions.

One of the reasons young people like suspense/adventure stories so much is that they're beginning to grow up. The search for suspense/adventure probably begins as soon as a child can crawl, because each new place to explore certainly becomes a suspense/adventure. Young people want to move away from the familiar to the unfamiliar. They want to confront the unknown and the difficult things of life.

A suspense/adventure may begin with any situation and in any setting, but often it's the story of someone's journey somewhere. Sometimes the journey is even internal, from fear to courage or from self-doubt to confidence.

Usually the most important element in a suspense/adventure story will be the suspense, and there are a couple of ways you can create it.

One way is to have a chase scene. In a chase, the main character is pursuing villains because they have something that he wants. Or you can reverse this and have the villains pursuing the main character because he has something that they want. In either case, you have a chase scene, which provides the tension in the story. Often in a suspense/adventure, the chase is the entire story. Other times, the chase is left until the end.

A second way to achieve suspense in a suspense/adventure story is to have a race against time. Here the young adventurer has only a set period of time in which to accomplish his goal. As the hours, the minutes, the seconds tick away, the terror mounts, because the young adventurer and the young reader both know just how much time is left. The question in both of their minds is, "Will I/he make it?"

The reader of a suspense/adventure story vicariously shares the experiences of the young adventurer as he gets in and out of scrapes, as he struggles to pull himself up to the summit of the mountain, as he struggles to climb a cliff, as he struggles against the current of a fast-moving river, as he struggles to outski a roaring avalanche. The young reader endures what the young adventurer endures. He's very excited about what's going to happen next and about how it'll happen. The young reader is constantly comparing what he would've done in a similar situation to what the young adventurer did.

It's up to the writer, then, to make sure that the hero is just a little better at figuring out what will come next than is the reader. The reader must always be just a little in awe of the young adventurer, but not so much in awe that he puts him on a pedestal and makes him seem entirely too perfect. The young adventurer needs to be somebody that the young reader would want to emulate, but usually not somebody who's so perfect that he'll stand out in a crowd as being superhuman or greatly different from everyone else. There must be enough difficult obstacles placed in front of the young adventurer that the reader will know deep down that he'll make it, although at the back of his mind will be the feeling that there's just a slim chance he might not!

You might wonder why suspense/adventure stories with

young people facing uncertainty and anxiety should be so popular with young people when they have to face uncertainty and anxiety every day. One reason is that the young adventurer in stories never fails to overcome the uncertainty and the anxiety. He always succeeds because of his sound judgment. The confidence that he has in himself always comes through. He's not afraid to take a chance if not doing so will mean failure. A good example of this type of character is Johnny Tremain in Esther Forbes' award-winning *Johnny Tremain*. While reading these stories, young readers often become paralyzed with excitement and perplexed as to what must be done to succeed. The young adventurer might become anxious or even frightened, but he'd never become paralyzed by fear (or anything else), because he's sure enough of himself not to. And this is indeed the greatest attraction for young people to suspense/adventure stories. Even though they're held in suspense for the length of the story, they know that in the end the young adventurer will overcome all obstacles and attain his goal and deliver them from their fear. The young adventurer, then, in a sense becomes a role model for all the daily adventures, no matter how mundane they might be, that each person has to face. The reader knows that if the young adventurer of the story he's just read can survive, he can survive, too.

As a beginning writer of suspense/adventure stories, you must remember that in a suspense/adventure story, the emphasis is on action. The young adventurer doesn't sit around exclaiming about the beauty of a rushing river; he swims across it. He doesn't extol the majesty of the surrounding mountains; he climbs them. He doesn't meditate about the beauty of the shifting desert sands; he crosses them. You must remember that the point of the suspense/adventure story is to have a suspenseful adventure while getting the young adventurer from one point to another.

A suspense/adventure story gives the reader a chance to escape into a scenario (as opposed to a fantasy) that, while it won't likely happen, *could* possibly happen. The reader must always feel that whatever takes place in a suspense/adventure story is within the realm of the possible.

There are really very few differences between the mystery

story and the suspense/adventure story, but the differences are fundamental. In a mystery, the crime or problem occurs right at the beginning; the hero spends the rest of the story trying to understand what's happened and who's responsible. In a suspense/adventure story, the crime or danger doesn't happen right away. It will be like a threatening thunderstorm just ready to break. The suspense comes from anticipating the crime or danger and from the excitement of wondering whether the hero will succeed in preventing or escaping it. The mystery story therefore looks mostly toward the recent past, figuring out what's happened and why, whereas the adventure/suspense story is concerned with the immediate future and what's going to happen next.

Another difference is that, in the mystery story, although the crime or problem is known, its meaning (and who's responsible) isn't revealed until the very end, as in "The Alphabet Letter Mystery" (pages 31-37), when the coded message is finally translated and the secret information recovered. In the suspense/adventure story, the hero generally knows who or what the danger is right away, and who the antagonist is, as in "Escape from East Berlin" (pages 178-182), when the young sisters are threatened by guards and rushing trains when, having lost their passports, they try to get back to West Berlin through the subway system.

Another difference is that, in the mystery story, the person who committed the crime isn't known until the very end of the story. In the suspense/adventure story, the person who committed the crime is known immediately, right at the beginning. The suspense/adventure comes in how he'll be captured.

The suspense/adventure story offers the writer a much wider range of possibilities than does the mystery story, because of the great many strictures of the latter. The suspense/adventure has no particular strictures that apply uniquely to it.

Here are some types of suspense/adventure stories you might want to consider if you're interested in writing this type of short story.

1. *The Kidnapping Story.* In this kind of suspense/ adventure story, a young person is kidnapped and uses his resources to outwit the kidnappers and find his way back home. This type of story offers the writer the opportunity to suggest ways a young person can avoid becoming a victim of a kidnapper.

2. The "Getting Back Home" Story. Often this type of story is a *part* of a suspense/adventure story, but sometimes it may provide the basis for the entire story. A young person could find himself cut off from his family during a camping trip in a forest, for example, and need to use his resources to find his way back. In this type of story, the reader isn't concerned with how the young person got lost, only with how he'll get back to home base.

3. The Alteration Story. This is one of the most exciting kinds of suspense/adventure stories for young people. It could probably better be handled in science fiction, but since it's such a fascinating adventure, I've included it here. In this type of story, a person becomes only an inch tall (or smaller, or even larger) and must survive in an entirely new environment. When I was young, I could sit for hours and think about what kind of world lay underneath the grass on our lawn. I could picture myself less than an inch tall, ready to set out into the "jungle" of our front lawn, ready to do battle with the insects and whatever else lay before me.

4. The Wolf-Boy Story. Even though this story has been told a thousand times, it's still a fascinating adventure for young people. In this type of story, a young person has been abandoned in the jungle and grows up among the animals. He's taken in, either by wolves, as in the traditional story, or by other animals, and he adapts to their ways. At some point in the story, the young person comes into contact with human beings and either decides to re-enter human society or stay where he is. This type of story, which has been done many times before, can still work if given a few fresh twists. A variation could be to substitute a primitive jungle tribe for animals and have the young person adapt to their ways. Yes, it, too, has been done, but it's still a fascinating adventure to young people, and it's just waiting for you to give it a new twist!

5. The Exploration Story.   In this type of story, a young person sets out to explore unknown territory (unknown at least to him). This can be a haunted house, an abandoned farm, a river, a national park, canyons close to home, or the streets of a big city. This story often embodies adventure for the sake of adventure. The young person pits himself against the unknown and sees if he can succeed in conquering it. It takes a lot of nerve for a young person (or even an older person) to explore a haunted house, but once he's done so, he's attained his goal and has grown in some way. (He may no longer be afraid of the dark, for example.)

If the young adventurer sets out to explore a national park, he may have to use his resources to find a cave to keep him safe from a raging blizzard; he may have to track his way through thick underbrush; he'll certainly have to find things to eat, so he'll have to search for wild fruits, berries, and nuts; he may have to escape the clutches of a bear or a mountain lion: but once he's reached his goal of having explored the national park, he'll no longer be the same person. He has survived by his wits and has grown.

6. The Fighting-the-Elements Story.   This is often a part of a greater suspense/adventure story, but it can in itself be the basis for an entire suspense/adventure story. In this type of story, the young adventurer must fight the elements in order to stay alive. The "elements" can be a hurricane, a snowstorm, an avalanche, a tornado—something usually to do with weather. The young adventurer can battle the sun, which will make him thirsty; the winds, which will dry out his body; a desert sandstorm, which will sting his eyes; or an ice storm, which will freeze him. In any of these situations, the young adventurer, if he's to survive, must prove his resourcefulness and think of things that will *allow* him to find a solution to his predicament.

7. The Disaster Story.   A disaster story is a survival story; it would be an excellent basis for a suspense/adventure story for young people. The disaster could be a shipwreck, a huge fire, or the crash of an airplane. In a disaster story, the young person would be primarily helping other people (and himself) survive.

51

8. The Detective Story. Most detective stories are handled under the mystery category, but if the crime is committed in the very beginning of the story and the criminal is known, then the story will be about how the detective goes about solving the case and catching the criminal, not about finding out who the criminal is.

9. The Sudden Terror Story. This is one of my favorite types of suspense/adventure stories. In a sudden terror story, an ordinary family is suddenly plunged into a terrifying situation by a series of events. They may be held hostage by escaped convicts or there may be somebody stalking them, calling them up on the telephone late at night and making threats. In other words, something terrible happens to them that plunges them into a state of terror. This is probably the most realistic of all the suspense/adventure types, because the characters are so ordinary. By ordinary, I don't mean they're uninteresting—I mean they're characters, usually a whole family, that anybody can identify with. In this type of story, a young member of the family is usually the one who comes up with the solution as to how to get rid of the escaped convicts (or whoever it is causing the family problems) without endangering the lives of his family.

10. The War Story. War stories are enjoyed by many young people, but the wars they enjoy reading about are World War II, the Civil War, and the American Revolution. Seldom is any other war or conflict used as the setting or basis for a war story for young people. If, however, you have a story idea that uses a different war, then by all means use it. I'm quite sure that, if it's well written, it'll interest an editor, because they do get tired of only three wars.

World War II offers endless possibilities for stories set in Jewish ghettos; stories of German young people finding Jewish refugees and hiding them (or arguing about what to do with them); stories of young people in Germany or other areas of occupied-Europe finding Allied soldiers and hiding them or helping them escape; stories of young people helping to deliver secret papers across enemy lines or under the noses of the Germans. World War II is still a romantic war to most adults and to young people who like to read war stories.

The Civil War and the American Revolution are also available to you as settings for war stories, mainly because of the popularity of *The Red Badge of Courage* and *Johnny Tremain*. These wars, in addition to similar story possibilities mentioned above for World War II, also offer the possibility of young people fighting as soldiers. The Civil War and the American Revolution will be covered further in the section on the historical story.

11. The Scientific Crisis Story. These suspense/adventure stories usually concern an impending disaster brought about by the release of a deadly virus or a germ. The toxic material has usually been stolen from a scientific laboratory. Again here, we're flirting with science fiction, but where the story belongs will depend on whether you emphasize the suspense/adventure part or the scientific part of the story.

In a scientific crisis story, the main characters can become directly involved in finding the lethal material, often without knowing exactly what it is. There may even be a character in the story who takes the material on purpose from a laboratory and thinks he's playing a harmless prank by letting it (a deadly virus, for instance) free.

12. The Spy Story. Young people enjoy spy stories because they almost always include secret codes and messages, and sometimes exciting chases. Chances are, however, it won't be your main character who'll be the spy. Newspapers are filled today with all sorts of spies, both from our country and from other countries. People spy for all kinds of reasons. A young person, for instance, might be living on a military post with his family and notice some suspicious characters. A young person might also become suspicious of the father or mother of a friend when he sees them handing over official-looking documents to another person. There are numerous possibilities for the spy story to become the basis of a suspense/adventure story for young people, including a story about rescuing somebody from enemy territory.

I'd now like for you to read one of my suspense/adventure stories, "Rescue in Hungary," a story in which somebody is rescued from enemy territory. Then I'll analyze it in light of the things I've just discussed.

RESCUE IN HUNGARY

BY GEORGE STANLEY

Allison Graham and her companion, Fejes Laszlo, were standing at the corner of Pietergasse and Feldstrasse in an almost deserted section of Vienna. It was 2 A.M. and the light from the streetlamp on the corner glistened off the wet cobblestones of the narrow streets.

Fejes was a student at the University of Vienna's medical school. She and her brother had escaped from Hungary two years earlier. Their father had been detained at the last minute and their mother had died three years before their escape.

Allison had met Fejes at the university when Allison's father, the noted epidemiologist, Dr. Edward Graham, had given a guest lecture. The girls had become fast friends, so close in fact that when Dr. Graham returned to the United States, Allison had stayed on with Fejes for the rest of the holiday vacation. The girls had made plans for a grand time together.

But Fejes's mood had changed two days ago after she had received an early morning telephone call. She became nervous and withdrawn. A second telephone call only hours before had brought them to where they now stood.

Allison looked at Fejes. "This is the stuff of spy novels," she said.

Fejes smiled. It was the first smile Allison had seen in several days.

"You may be right," Fejes said, then turned again to look down the deserted street.

Allison looked too. In the distance, she saw the headlights of a slowly moving car.

Fejes tensed as the headlights appeared larger.

"Here," Fejes whispered and pulled Allison into the shadows of a nearby building. The stone felt cold and clammy against Allison's arm. As the car drew closer, Fejes stepped away from the building.

The car stopped. It was a Russian make, Allison noticed. A man rolled down the window. "Get in," he said.

Fejes did as she was told. Allison hesitated. Although she trusted Fejes, she was not in the habit of getting into cars with strangers, especially at 2 A.M. on a deserted street in Vienna, Austria.

Fejes looked up at Allison. "It's all right," she called softly. "This is my Uncle Jozsef."

Allison climbed in beside Fejes and the car sped away.

They had been driving for fifteen minutes before Uncle Jozsef spoke.

"It's about your father," he said.

Fejes made a choking sound, but said nothing. Allison saw tears in her eyes.

"Is he bad?" Fejes finally asked.

"I don't know," said Uncle Jozsef. "But I think so. Yes."

"Haven't you taken him to the hospital?" There was a note of hysteria in Fejes's question.

Uncle Jozsef's frown deepened. "We can't."

"Why not?" asked Fejes.

"He's wanted by the secret police, that's why," replied Uncle Jozsef. "No doctor in Hungary will touch him. If we tried to take him to the hospital, he would be arrested and put into prison."

Fejes put her hand over her mouth and stifled a sob. Finally she asked, "What's going to happen to him?"

"He'll die unless something is done," replied Uncle Jozsef.

"Then I'll go to him," said Fejes determinedly.

"He doesn't want you to come," said Jozsef. "You don't know how proud he is of you and what you're doing. It's been one of the things that has kept him alive, knowing that one day you'll become a doctor."

"I must go. I can't let him die."

"Listen, Fejes, if you're caught, you'll be shot!" said Uncle Jozsef. "There is a price on your head too."

Fejes turned suddenly to Allison. "What am I to do?" Tears were streaming down her face. "I can't let my father die."

56

Allison took a deep breath, then exhaled. "I will go for you," she said.

"Oh, I can't let you do that!" said Fejes. "You could not take such a risk."

Uncle Jozsef was shaking his head. "Do you realize, my dear girl, that I am here only because I have knowledge of the border zone? I knew the area well before it was sealed off. I know how to get through the mines and the barbed wire, although even I am taking a chance. But *two* of us, at night! No, no."

"I believe you, Uncle Jozsef," said Allison, "but I'm willing to risk it."

"Oh, Allison," Fejes cried, "I'd be eternally grateful to you! I can get some medical supplies at the university, things that I'm sure would help you."

"It's settled, then," said Allison. "We leave for Hungary as soon as possible."

There remained a grim expression on Uncle Jozsef's face as he nodded but said nothing.

***

By the next evening Fejes had collected a black bag full of medical supplies for Allison. After a late and solemn dinner, Allison and Uncle Jozsef bid Fejes good-bye and left for the Hungarian border.

They drove southeast from Vienna, following roads that led them through no large towns, only small villages, until they reached a heavily wooded area where Uncle Jozsef stopped the car.

"The border zone is about a mile over that way," he said, pointing. "And a mile beyond that is the village of Koszeg. That's where we're going."

Allison could feel her heart pounding. She had known danger before, but nothing like this. There would be mines planted that would explode with the slightest pressure. There would be guards patrolling with dogs trained to kill. And high up in the towers there would be other guards with searchlights and machine guns.

"Are you ready?" asked Uncle Jozsef.

Allison inhaled sharply. "I'm ready," she said.

They started walking. Allison carried the black bag with the medical supplies. Just a few yards from the car, Allison stumbled and fell against Uncle Jozsef.

"That could be fatal," he whispered, "once we get into the zone. A stumble could trip a wire or trigger a mine."

"I know," said Allison. "I'm sorry."

"There's nothing to be sorry about," said Uncle Jozsef. "Just be more careful, that's all."

Suddenly they were through the woods and into a clearing.

"We're here," whispered Uncle Jozsef, stopping. "Follow me closely."

They started walking again. Slowly. Slowly.

"Down!" whispered Uncle Jozsef urgently. Allison fell to the ground as a searchlight passed over them.

"Up, quickly, Allison!" It was almost a hiss.

They were walking faster now, and it scared Allison. But she had faith in Uncle Jozsef. She had to.

And then she heard them. The dogs. Their growls were horrible sounds, and seemed to be getting closer.

Uncle Jozsef said nothing, but he quickened his pace.

They were moving fast. Then she stumbled. The black bag went flying out of her hands, spilling open. There were tinkling sounds as the glass tubes and bottles hit the ground.

Uncle Jozsef stopped and pulled her up. Holding tightly onto her hand, he started through the zone.

"Wait!"she whispered desperately, "the bag, the medicine, we need to save what we can!"

"There's not time! Can't you hear them?"

She could hear them. The dogs. They were getting closer, their growls more and more terrifying.

"But we must," Allison pleaded.

"If we save the medicine, we kill ourselves. Which do you want?"

But Uncle Jozsef gave her no time to answer. He tightened his grip on Allison's hand and they began running through the zone. A searchlight passed over them, but they didn't stop, and finally they reached the barbed wire. Uncle Jozsef bent down and pulled it up just far enough so that Allison could crawl under it. When she was through, Allison held the wire up for Uncle Jozsef. His shirt caught, but he ripped free.

When he was up, he grabbed her hand again. They ran until they had reached the woods. Only then did he slow his pace to a walk, and Allison was able to get her breath.

58

"We're far enough from the zone that we can rest a moment," Uncle Jozsef said, "but not for long. They patrol this area too, sometimes."

Allison felt the night air and for a moment thought it was freezing her skin. "How far are we from Koszeg?" she asked.

"It's just over there," replied Uncle Jozsef, "beyond those trees. We may be able to see a light or two but not much more."

"Where's Fejes's father?" asked Allison.

"Tamas is living in the cellar of a cousin's house just outside the village. He's been living there for a year."

"Why hasn't he escaped before?" she asked.

"The time was never right. It's that simple. He had a good job as a newspaper editor. He was always watched, but he was relatively safe."

"What happened to change that?" Allison asked.

"He angered the wrong people, that's all. His newspaper was closed. His property was seized. He was to be put on trial, but he escaped. He has been hiding in Anna Buda's cellar ever since. Come on, it's time to go."

They followed a dirt road that went directly past the cousin's house. Uncle Jozsef walked up to the door of the farmhouse and knocked lightly. Allison stood beside him. It was several minutes before the door opened. The old woman didn't seem too happy to see them.

"What is wrong, Anna?" Uncle Jozsef asked.

"It's Tamas," she said. "He's crazy. He was screaming last night. I can't have that, Jozsef. There were some soldiers here at noon yesterday. They just asked for water, but they could have heard him if he had screamed while they were here! Then where would I be? I'm too old for prison, Jozsef. I want to spend my last days in peace."

"Could we see him?" Allison asked.

Anna looked at Allison, seemingly for the first time. Then she went to a drawer and took out a ring of large keys.

"I had to lock him in," she said. "It was for his own good."

Allison and Uncle Jozsef followed Anna to the cellar. Allison looked at the sky. In a few hours, it would be dawn. She realized how useless her visit was now—with the medical supplies scattered somewhere out in the zone. She wondered if the soldiers had found them yet.

Anna unlocked and opened the door to the cellar. "After you

go in, I'll close it," said Anna, "but I won't lock it if you'll promise to keep him quiet."

"We promise," Allison said.

Allison and Uncle Jozsef stepped inside and carefully went down the steps. In a corner a small paraffin lamp was lit, and on a small cot lay a frail-looking man.

Allison went over and felt his forehead. It was extremely hot. The man moaned.

His shirt was open, and Allison noticed some rose-colored eruptions on his chest. His pulse was very weak.

"Can you tell what is wrong with him?" Uncle Jozsef asked.

Allison hesitated. If it was what she thought it was, Uncle Jozsef would probably refuse to do what she had in mind. "I'm not sure at this point," she said, "but I do know that if we don't get him to a doctor quickly he will die."

"He will die if he sees a doctor," said Uncle Jozsef. "The authorities want him, and they are watching everybody."

"Then we must take him back to Austria," said Allison firmly.

"Are you crazy?"

"You're strong," said Allison. "And he's small and frail. You could carry him."

"But . . ."

"We'll go back the same way we came," Allison continued. "I'll lead the way. Surely they won't expect anyone to use the same route for escape."

Uncle Jozsef thought for a minute, then let out a sigh. "You're right. He is my brother, and I cannot leave him here to die."

"We'll leave as soon as it's dark enough," Allison said. "Meanwhile, let's make him as comfortable as possible and get some rest ourselves."

***

It was nearing midnight when Allison and Uncle Jozsef finally left the cellar. Anna was glad to see them go, although she said nothing. Allison could see it in her eyes.

Uncle Jozsef carried Tamas over his shoulder. Allison led them along the road from Anna's house. They stopped twice to hide while military vehicles were passing. Allison tried not to think of the danger that lay ahead of them. Finally, they reached the wooded area where they had rested the night before. They needed a short rest now before they went into the zone.

They had rested for only ten minutes when Tamas started shaking.

"He's getting chilled," said Allison. "We must hurry."

Uncle Jozsef picked Tamas up. They left the protection of the trees and started toward the zone. Almost immediately they saw the beam of a searchlight and fell to the ground. The light hesitated for a few seconds before it passed on.

"Let's wait a minute," whispered Uncle Jozsef. And suddenly the searchlight appeared over them again. "They probably thought they saw something."

Tamas moaned. Uncle Jozsef put his hand over Tamas' mouth to stifle the sound.

When they were satisfied that it was safe to get up, they continued, reaching the barbed wire faster than Allison had thought they would.

Allison pulled the wire up so Uncle Jozsef could crawl underneath it. Then, with Allison's help, Uncle Jozsef dragged Tamas underneath. Finally, it was Allison's turn.

Uncle Jozsef hoisted Tamas onto his shoulders again and began following Allison through the mine fields.

With no moon, it was much darker than the night before. They were in the mine fields, and she couldn't see where she was going! Uncle Jozsef bumped into her and stopped.

"We're in trouble," she whispered. "I can't see where I'm going."

"I think we're in the same place as last night," said Uncle Jozsef. "Walk in as straight a direction as you can. We don't have too much farther to go."

Allison turned and started walking. She had taken no more than three steps when her foot tripped a wire. The scream of sirens seemed to surround them. Searchlights began coming on. And then she heard the growls of the dogs.

"Run!" shouted Uncle Jozsef.

He had taken the lead now and was running through the field, Tamas bouncing up and down on his shoulder. Allison was behind him. Bursts of machine-gun fire exploded in the night.

Allison ran until she thought she could run no more, and it was only when she saw Uncle Jozsef fall to the ground, Tamas with him, that she realized that the sounds were all far behind.

"We're through," Uncle Jozsef gasped. "We made it!" Tears

streamed down his face.

Allison fell down beside him. She felt like crying too. Then Tamas's moaning caught her attention.

"We must find the car," she said quickly.

They found the road on which they had left the car, then a hundred yards beyond, they found the car. Allison helped Uncle Jozsef put Tamas into the back seat, and she covered him with a blanket.

They both hurriedly got into the car. Uncle Jozsef started the engine, and they sped off into the night toward Vienna.

"We must get Tamas to a doctor as quickly as possible," said Allison. "I didn't want to alarm you earlier, but I'm almost positive that he has *typhoid fever.*"

THE SUSPENSE SHORT STORY

"Rescue in Hungary" appeared in both *Jr. Medical Detective* and *Health Explorer*. It was a story from my Allison Graham series.

The first thing I'd like to point out is that the story is set in a foreign country. You'll often hear that editors don't like to buy stories that are set in foreign countries because young people don't like to read them. There's probably some truth to this, but I think that the eight-to-twelve age group *will* read stories set somewhere else besides the United States. For one thing, they're studying other countries in school and are usually interested in finding out more about them. It's obvious that *some* editors do buy *some* stories set in foreign countries. In fact, you can probably set your stories in foreign countries much more easily than you can your novels.

In "Rescue from Hungary," Allison Graham will be testing her wits against the border guards at the Austrian-Hungarian frontier. She's motivated by a desire to save the father of her friend, Fejes. In order to reach her goal, she'll have to overcome the following obstacles:

1. the barbed wire at the border
2. the buried land mines
3. the border guards
4. the guard dogs
5. the searchlights

In the story, Allison and Fejes's Uncle Jozsef successfully conquer these opposing forces and slip into Hungary, but they know and the reader knows that they'll also have to conquer these same forces in order to get out.

Allison is afraid, her heart is pounding, but what is important is that hers is a healthy fear, not a paralyzing fear. She has looked the enemy straight in the eye and said that she knows the obstacles she faces are great but that her cause is greater, and she'll overcome these obstacles. Allison Graham, therefore, has earned the respect of the reader because she's literally put her life on the line for someone she's never met.

In "Rescue in Hungary," Allison Graham demonstrates that she's strong and resourceful. She has taken a physical endurance test and has passed.

Allison possesses a special sensitivity that will allow her to outguess her opponents. When Allison is faced with a decision regarding what to do with Tamas, she decides to take him back to Austria, although she knows the almost impossibility of accomplishing this task. Uncle Jozsef thinks she's crazy, but she tells him that they'll go back the same way they came, because the authorities won't be expecting that.

It's this solid determination to overcome these obstacles that places Allison Graham just slightly above the reader. She'll not waver from her goals until they've been reached, even though it means that she might lose her life (which, of course, seldom happens in these stories).

On the journey back to Austria, this time with Fejes's father, Allison and Uncle Jozsef have to:

1. keep Tamas from screaming out

2. dodge searchlights

3. crawl underneath barbed wire

4. pull Tamas underneath the same barbed wire

5. walk through mine fields

After Allison has accidentally tripped a wire, she and Uncle Jozsef have to:

6. dodge more searchlights

7. escape from the guard dogs

8. dodge machine-gun bullets

until they finally reach the Austrian border and have successfully accomplished their goal of *rescuing somebody from enemy territory.*

5

The Science Fiction Short Story

When I was growing up, I used to lie on the warm sidewalk in front of our house in the small town of Memphis, Texas, during the summer and look up at the stars, hoping I'd see a flying saucer. This was a time of UFO sightings. It was before man had ever walked on the moon and a time when that reality had not yet spoiled the creativity of the young. This was a time of outer space movies and incredible-looking monsters. It was a time, at least for me, of a more innocent type of science fiction, a science fiction that maybe the purists don't care for, but a science fiction that interested a lot of people.

Although this type of science fiction may have been tempered somewhat by both man and real rocket ships making trips to the moon and beyond, these accomplishments certainly haven't diminished the interest of young people in science fiction. If they've done anything, they've sharpened it and made it seem more like fact than fiction.

More than in any other category, a story's background is the most important element in science fiction. The fortunate thing for a writer is that since the story usually takes place in the future, the background can be composed almost entirely from the writer's imagination.

I think one of the key words to remember when writing science fiction is *vision*. As a science fiction writer, you need a very keen eye for what might be. You must remember that you are, in essence, the creator of a new world.

Following are the three periods in which you can set science fiction stories for young people:

1. the present

2. the near future

3. the distant future

When most people think of the present, they don't think of science fiction. In fact, I much prefer my science fiction stories set in the present. One of my favorite science fiction television series, "The Invaders," was about a man in the present who witnessed the landing of a flying saucer and knew that aliens had invaded the earth. He spent the rest of the series looking for these aliens and trying to convince people that there really were aliens who had invaded the earth. Nothing in the everyday lives of the people in the series was different from that of the people watching the series, except for the fact that they were surrounded by aliens. But even the aliens looked like human beings, and the only way you could tell the difference was by examining an alien's little finger. It wouldn't line up straight next to the ring finger—it stuck out some. It absolutely scared me to death when the main character would suddenly notice this abnormality, usually on a person he'd been trusting for most of the show. Things like that have always scared me much more than some odd-colored, strange-looking, rubber-masked, inhuman-like creature.

There's another science fiction film set in the present that I've always enjoyed immensely. In *Invasion of The Body Snatchers*, pods from outer space are deposited on earth and duplicate the bodies of ordinary people. Everything else in the lives of the characters is normal.

The present is always a good starting point for beginning writers of science fiction. First of all, I think it's scarier to think of things like what's happening in these two stories happening to us in our ordinary lives than it is the possibility of journeying to a distant planet. Too, the amount of research on world-creation is negligible, compared to what other science fiction stories can require. There are many young people who, as I did, find other science fiction stories too farfetched.

Another time frame for your science fiction story can be the near future. The near future can be ten, twenty, thirty, perhaps even forty years from now. Of the three time frames, this can be the most difficult, because the setting shouldn't be totally created from the imagination of the writer. It's important to realize that even young readers of science fiction have a pretty good idea of what scientists are doing now and what they might accomplish in ten, twenty, thirty, or even forty years. There must be some connection between the time in which the reader is now living and the near future, in which the story is set. This calls for a fair amount of research on the part of the writer. Of course, even in extrapolating a possible near future time frame from the present world, you're able to go many different directions, so there are endless possibilities for creativity. Following are some things you might want to consider:

1. What kinds of houses would people be living in?

2. What kinds of clothes would they wear?

3. What kinds of food would they eat?

4. What kinds of automobiles would they be driving?

5. What kinds of other transportation would they use?

6. What kinds of schools would the young people go to?

7. What kinds of books would everyone read? (Would people even read?)

8. What kinds of entertainment would everyone be interested in?

9. What kinds of jobs would people have?

There are many more questions that you could answer to help create the kind of background in which your story characters would exist, but these are some of the major ones to be considered.

You should be familiar enough with the setting of your story that you could pass an examination on it. Some writers keep detailed notebooks that read almost like current geography texts, in which they write out detailed answers to these and other questions. The length of your short story will probably determine just how detailed you can be; however, it's still important that you establish your background well—even if you end up not using all the material—so that you don't make a mistake and have your characters doing things that they couldn't possibly do.

The third time frame in which you can set a science fiction story is the distant future. If you set your story in a time period that's several centuries, not just several decades, from now, then you will have almost limitless freedom in your creativity. Nobody can say how the world will be several hundred years from now, so your guess is as good as anybody else's. Research is almost unnecessary for this time frame. The only thing you have to remember is that you should be consistent in the detailing of your background. Again, you shouldn't have your main characters doing things that you've not allowed for in this detailing.

Once you've decided upon your time-frame background, you're ready to develop your story plot. It's always a good idea to have at least a germ of an idea for a story before you've chosen your time-frame background, since they'll affect each other.

Following are discussions of the types of science fiction plots that you can use for your stories:

1. *The If-This-Goes-On Story.* This is probably one of the story types that will attract the most attention from young readers, because it can deal with something that possibly could affect them in their day-to-day lives. In fact, they may already be concerned with it, and your job is to project it into their future, where it'll become not just an interest or an irritant but the whole focus of their lives.

I live in a part of the country that sees very high temperatures in late July and August. During this time of the year, the temperature often soars past the 100 degrees Fahrenheit mark and stays there, sometimes for weeks at a time. Most people are used to it—very few actually think any more about it than that it's awfully hot. But if the extreme heat does linger longer than usual, if the power stations begin experiencing brownouts or blackouts and people aren't able to use their air conditioners much, if the lakes, which are the local water sources, begin to dry up, then some people do start thinking, what will happen . . *if this goes on?*

What if the end of August comes and the temperature doesn't come down but continues to rise? What if the schools open and the rooms are worse than ovens? What if September ends and the temperature continues to soar? *What if this goes on?* It's frightening to contemplate, but what if it did continue to get hotter and hotter—what would happen? What would the world be like? How would people adapt? Would living on earth become like living on one of the planets that we know has surface temperatures of several thousand degrees? Of course, the converse of this could be, what if it got colder and colder? What would *that* be like and how would people survive?

Quite often, these types of stories serve as good warning stories. You might also consider stories about overpopulation, nuclear energy, contamination of food and water sources—almost any subject that you think we don't pay enough attention to. The one thing you do need to avoid in this type of story is preachiness. You want to make sure that you're first and foremost telling a good story. If your story has a lesson, as does "Forbidden Knowledge" by Cynthia Wall, at the end of this chapter, then it'll still come through. In fact, it will be remembered much longer than if the reader thinks the story is simply an excuse for you to put across your opinion on the subject.

It's very important to remember in this type of story that the element you're focusing on will affect every other element of society, so you'll at least have to touch on these elements. Decide before you start how the continued rise in the temperature, for instance, will affect:

1. attending school

2. family relationships

3. fire and police protection

4. clothing

5. the houses people live in

6. the food people eat

7. playing with friends

You would have to understand and consider all of these things and others before you could write a good "If this goes on . . ." type of story.

2. The Alien Contact Story.   Basically, an alien contact story is one in which only a few people, perhaps even one person, know that the earth has been invaded by alien beings. The basic job of these people (and the plot of the story) is to convince the rest of the world that there are indeed aliens on earth.

The alien contact story can, however, also include stories about people from earth journeying to distant or unknown planets and coming in contact with aliens, either friendly or hostile. The movie *Aliens* shows a hostile meeting; in *E. T.,* the alien is friendly—it's people who are dangerous.

If you choose the aliens-coming-to-earth story, you must have a reason for the visit. Maybe it's just a scientific expedition, as in *E. T.* Or maybe something is going wrong on the aliens' planet and they're seeking new territory. Maybe their planet's problem could affect our planet next. Maybe the water is totally polluted and the aliens—like us—can't exist without water. Again, this type of story can often serve as a reminder to young people that if we all don't take care of our planet, we, too, might be forced to leave it and find a new environment. (Probably, in order for your story to be realistic, you'll need to thoroughly research science textbooks to see what actually happens when the environment is mistreated and goes haywire.) The aliens' coming to earth can be friendly or hostile on their part. Similarly, it can be viewed by earthlings as either friendly or hostile. If your characters come from a planet totally different from earth, you'll generally have to do a great deal of research to determine the different things that exist on other planets and what types of beings would be found there.

If, on the other hand, your alien beings come from a planet similar to earth, there would be very little need for research, because you could simply describe how you yourself exist in earth's environment.

You'll need to decide whether you'll handle your alien characters as serious characters or as comic characters. In many of the recent science-fiction films, a lot of the aliens have been comic characters. They made us laugh in addition to thrilling us. I don't particularly like comic science-fiction characters, but that's my preference; still, I think it shows that you shouldn't try to use characters that you *aren't* sympathetic to. My preference could stem from my enjoying being scared out of my wits. If I'm confronted by strange-looking or comic characters, I don't take the story seriously. You must remember that some of your readers will react in this way, too. I like for my aliens to look similar to the way I look, but to have one little abnormality (not readily apparent) that points to them as being aliens. It's always chilling to me to see this abnormality and to be caught unaware, thinking that I (and the main character) have been associating with a perfectly normal earthling.

3. The Time Machine Story. Although adults may no longer care for this type of story, it's still a favorite with young people, who still fantasize about machines that can take them back

71

in time. There are still a lot of story lines available for the beginning writer to come up with all sorts of new ways that a person can go back in time. A recent motion picture had a young man traveling back in time to see his parents as teenagers. This is something a lot of teenagers would like to do. This story attracted a very large audience, showing that time travel still interests young people, provided the story is presented with a new twist.

One of the reasons that this type of story is so popular is that it doesn't take a lot of scientific explanation to discuss seconds, minutes, hours, days—even years or centuries. This is something that people understand. They also understand the past and the future. And since time travel is really something that has never been accomplished, the field is open to all sorts of creative ways to have characters travel in time.

There probably isn't a young person alive who hasn't at one time or another wanted to visit another time period. Perhaps he's just read a story about some historical event and said, *I wish I could have watched that take place.* In a time-travel story, he can. He can actually put himself in another time period, whether it be past or future.

Trips into the future require the same type of research that I've already discussed. You need to make sure that if you're dealing with the near future, what's happening in your story could possibly happen. You must reasonably extrapolate the information from your research. If your main character is traveling to a time in the distant future, then you'll have more flexibility. If he's traveling back in time, then you'll need to do background research on the historical event. Even if you plan to have your main character change the past, so that the future will change, you need to make sure that the past is correctly represented before you decide to change it.

I should give you a word of warning here about tampering with the past, the present, or the future. Things tend to get rather complicated fast. If your main character decides to *change* the past rather than simply observe it, then he (and you) will need to realize that all the changes he makes will affect generations of people. If you start taking stock of all the things that would have to be changed if you disturb the past, then you might want to think twice before you have your main character do anything other than simply observe it.

The same holds true for trips into the future. What if your main character sees something happening to his family or to a friend or to a friend's family? Will you have your main character change that? And how will that change affect future generations? All these things have to be considered. Of course, this thinking on the part of the main character that he'll be able to change the past or the future is one of the reasons this type of story is so attractive to young people. It's part of the thrill of reading it and the daydreaming afterwards.

4. The Scientific-Discovery Story. Young people are always inventing in their minds new devices that'll change the world and make *their* lives more interesting and easier. You can take advantage of these mind inventions and invent your own scientific discovery that will revolutionize their lives. Your story will detail the effects that the new discovery will have on their lives. It can be a device that will help them pass examinations without studying, or cause them to become invisible so they can go places they ordinarily wouldn't be allowed to go. When I was growing up, I kept wanting something that would make me invisible so I could go into the two movie theaters in my home town and watch movies any time I wanted to. (Actually, I still wish I had such a device in order to do the same thing now!)

These types of inventions can be comic; usually, the inventions used in a scientific-discovery story for young people are comic, not serious—although you can certainly invent something serious that'll change your main character's life. You could invent a device that would keep people from hating each other, or a means of producing all the food the world needs, or a way to purify ocean water *simply* and *cheaply*. A look in almost any science textbook will give you some idea of the things that need to be done, or perhaps things that science is now trying to do (such as finding cures for all the diseases in the world), in order to create a better world.

73

5. The "Journey through a Strange Land" Story.
This, too, is a very popular type of story for young people, although it's been done in stories, books, and films on a number of occasions. In this type of story, several young people could be taking a hike through some canyons, come upon a cave, enter the cave, and find a back exit that opens onto a strange world. Young people are fascinated by other worlds. One of the reasons this type of story is so popular is that it offers a young person a chance to do something that might possibly happen. Since space travel isn't involved, only ordinary hiking, there's always the possibility, they fantasize, that just beyond the next cliff or just over the next rise, they'll come upon a strange and exciting new world. I've often experienced this same sensation when hiking. Just as I reach the bottom of a cliff, I see through a formation of the land a small area, an oasislike area, that seems out of place. It's then that the sensation of having discovered another world, a place that maybe nobody else has ever seen, strikes me. Such a place, then, is the basis for this type of story.

The characters in a journey-through-a-strange-land story always start at Point A and plan to journey to Point Z, but somewhere along the way, they travel through a land that's strangely different from the one they've just left. The plants are different; the animals are different; the people are different. Often in stories of this kind, the main characters travel back to a lost world, a world of dinosaurs and other prehistoric creatures, but the setting can actually be any type of land you choose. You, the writer, must make sure, however, that you keep your characters moving. They usually can't go back the way they came because the entrance becomes blocked in some way, often by a rockslide, forcing your main characters to make their journey through this strange land in hopes of finding another way out. Remember, the emphasis in this type of story is on the journey. That's the reason you must keep your characters moving. Your main characters may come in contact with aliens, but the aliens would merely be *one* of the components of the story, not the main component, as they would be in an alien contact story.

Probably more than any other category, science fiction

changes with each new scientific discovery. Young people will be interested in it, though, as long as there are warm summer sidewalks on which to lie while looking up into the stars.

I'd now like for you to read "Forbidden Knowledge," an if-this-goes-on story by Cynthia Wall, and then I'll analyze it.

Forbidden Knowledge

BY CYNTHIA WALL

From a distance the Earth's control center resembled a hive of bees anxiously tending its Queen Mother. Beneath the dome of synthetic steel and glass lay Rega, the command computer. From its complex programs came instructions which ran lesser centers around the world.

The one million scientists who lived at the Rega Center were kept busy maintaining the systems. In a sense, Rega was a mother to them all. From the huge clock on the dome ceiling—which read 8:30, 11 March 2081—to the small calculator each scientist carried, everything was run from the power and programs made by Rega.

In classroom 2036, programs designed to train the scientists' children in this important work flashed on the wall. XY10019 took her lessons seriously. She would be twelve on her next birthday. She had learned every procedure the training calculators and computers were capable of teaching her. In time she would replace her father in the actual care of Rega.

The number sequences on the wall ended, and XY10019 stood up to stretch. She had free time until midday nourishment, and she quickly went outside the center. She ran along the quiet streets until she reached the woods at the south end. With a backward glance to make sure no one was watching, she slipped into the cool darkness of the forest.

"Michael," she called softly. The tall slender boy who appeared at the edge of the clearing was similar in size to XY10019. He was clothed only in animal skins in sharp contrast to XY10019's pale gray uniform.

"Hi," Michael said. "You're just in time. Grandfather will be starting the lesson soon."

The two friends hurried across a small meadow and into deeper woods on the other side. XY10019 felt the same thrill of secrecy she always did when entering this forbidden area.

Michael was a member of one of the few families of savages yet remaining on Earth. The center civilization had long ago given up capturing these people who insisted on maintaining their primitive ways. A humanitarian movement within the center had convinced the leaders to ignore the savages. They caused no one harm, and the center felt certain they would die out in a period of years.

XY10019 had met Michael quite by chance years ago while she was walking in the woods. Michael had been playing a strange game with pebbles in the dirt when XY10019 came upon him. After a quick greeting, the two had settled down to play together. From that first game a friendship had blossomed.

She had known better than to tell her parents where she went each day on her walks, because talking with the savages was forbidden.

Now as she followed Michael into the cave where he lived with his family, she felt excitement for Grandfather's lesson. She knew from hearing the elders talk at the center that the simple things Michael's grandfather was teaching them had once been common knowledge. But with the use of calculators and computers, such teaching had been declared useless and forbidden more than sixty years ago.

Still XY10019 found the lessons fascinating, and she was always sorry when the hour drew to a close. Today was no exception.

After the lesson she bid Michael good-bye and walked through the woods toward the center.

She was admiring a wild lily at the edge of the forest when the first tremor struck. She stared in disbelief as the streets of the center crumpled before her eyes. The middle portion of the dome was collapsing, and she could hear ominous crunching sounds from the portion of the center located underground.

The ground was lurching violently, and she heard the cracking of trees behind her. She crawled to an open space and lay flat on the ground. The frenzied rocking seemed to continue for an eternity, and she closed her eyes and ears to the horrible sights and screams in front of her.

Finally, when the quaking slowed, she got up and made her

way on unsteady feet to the rubble that had once been the Rega Center.

For days XY10019 helped carry the injured clear of the wreckage. Once she thought she saw Michael and his father tending a dying woman, but her eyes were too tired to be sure.

Miraculously her own parents had been spared, but many of her friends and relatives had not. When it was over and the dead were all buried, she sat in on a conference of the remaining scientists.

"It is finished," her father said solemnly. "Rega has been destroyed. The other centers in the world are no longer receiving energy. All of our instruments are useless. Even if we could manufacture our food, which we can't, we would die without shelter when winter comes."

XY10019 listened intently and made a motion as if to speak. Her father silenced her with a stern look. But one of the elders said, "Let the girl speak."

"Well," she began hesitantly, "why couldn't we rebuild the center? Why couldn't we rebuild Rega?"

"Child!" the elder laughed. "Rebuild? How? Rega has always programmed machines to manufacture materials needed for new buildings. Then they have been automatically assembled by other machines programmed by her. Without Rega we are helpless."

"But," XY10019 interrupted impatiently, "couldn't we build a dome like this?" She squatted down and sketched some shapes in the dust on a broken piece of steel.

"Where did you learn how to do that?" the scientists gasped in unison.

"From the savages," she admitted sheepishly. "I also know how to grow food from the earth."

The sun rose early the next morning as did XY10019. The dust from the quake was still settling, and an occasional aftershock sent small columns of it drifting up toward the sky.

XY10019, followed by the leaders of the center, walked slowly to the woods. Michael met them in the clearing.

"We thought you would be coming," he said softly.

His grandfather was standing beside him, and he put a compass, a ruler, and some counting beads down on the ground. The men sat down in a circle, and Grandfather began the lesson.

78

I think "Forbidden Knowledge" is an excellent example of an if-this-goes-on story, because it shows what can happen if a society continues to let machines do most of their thinking for them: "From (Rega's) complex programs came instructions which ran lesser centers around the world." The great minds of the society, the one million scientists who lived at the Rega Center, didn't think. They only maintained the systems. They *attended* the giant computer, much like the worker bees attend the Queen Bee.

I see an interesting parallel today in the problem of memorizing multiplication tables versus the use of calculators in classrooms. There are many students who see absolutely no reason at all to memorize multiplication tables, because they think they'll always have a calculator at hand—much like the scientists in "Forbidden Knowledge" think that Rega will always be there.

Although "Forbidden Knowledge" is set a few years beyond what is normally considered the near future, I'd still classify it as a near-future story, because readers will find it easy to extrapolate from the present to the time of the story, the year 2081.

Ms. Wall has created a vivid science fiction setting by contrasting such things as (1) the domed world of the computer with familiar quiet streets and a woods at the south end (of the town); (2) the pale gray school uniform of XY10019 with Michael's animal skins; and (3) the school of the future with the school of the savages.

All in all, Cynthia Wall has produced an excellent picture of what our world might become "if this goes on." Young people reading this story can see that a more technical world is not necessarily a better world, if fundamental knowledge is forgotten or *forbidden*.

6

The Fantasy Short Story

What is fantasy? Fantasy is the literature of both good and bad magic; it has some of the characteristics of a dream. It's the story of gnarled trees and black forests, of little creatures whose eyes glow in the dark as they peer out at us from underneath leaves and toadstools. There's a certain strangeness to fantasy, at once frightening but still compelling, drawing us into it.

The most important thing a writer can do in fantasy is to make his reader believe in what's happening. Of course, what the writer is actually asking the reader to do is suspend disbelief. But fantasy must also be logical: a fantasy world must have its rules and regulations just like any other world. They may be *fantastic* rules and regulations, but the inhabitants of the fantasy world must abide by them.

Fantasy, good fantasy, isn't very easy to write, although

many beginning writers seem to think it is; and frankly, from what editors tell me, it's even harder to sell. Many editors cringe when they hear the word *fantasy,* because they've received some absolutely awful fantasy stories over the years and they don't particularly feel like seeing any more; so it's up to you to make sure that the fantasy story you're writing can compare with some of the best. (Read Zilpha Keatley Snyder's *The Changeling,* a story about a girl who claims to be the child of supernatural parents; Susan Cooper's five-book series named *The Dark Is Rising,* the theme of which is the complicated, ageless conflict between good and evil, the Light and the Dark; and Mary Rogers' *Freaky Friday,* in which a teenager turns into her mother, and her mother turns into her—for one hilarious day!)

This attitude on the part of many editors toward fantasy has in fact become so strong that many market reports will indicate that no fantasy will be accepted. The actual fact is that you may still be able to interest an editor in fantasy, but you'll probably have to approach him through a well-written query letter that assures him of the quality of your fantasy. What editors often mean when they say they don't want to see any fantasy is that they don't want to see any more poorly written fantasies that are easily recognizable as retellings of the Brothers Grimm or Hans Christian Andersen.

For many people, fantasy is a type of story that is totally irrelevant to the real world and as such doesn't belong to a period in which people have given up dreaming. Fantasy is, for the most part, a literature dealing with magic and the supernatural. Unlike science fiction, it isn't based on scientific research and extrapolation. Fantasy requires that we suspend disbelief, and it requires a great amount of faith on the part of the reader—more than that required by any of the other categories. A good example is "No Cows in the City" by Carol H. Behrman. There are no explanations for all the outlandish things that the cow in the story does, and the result is pure fantasy that reads like a straight story.

The minute you begin to explain why something is happening in your story, you're no longer writing fantasy, you're writing science fiction; this is one of the main differences between the two categories. Another and perhaps related difference is that in fantasy, magic and the supernatural are often assumed to exist, whereas in science fiction, everything is assumed to conform to ordinary natural laws, even in those cases where it's not actually explained. Or, to put it another way, in science fiction, events are *explainable,* even if not explained. In fantasy, they're not. Now let's look at some of the similarities.

Fantasy and science fiction are usually set in similar times and places that are either alien or quite different from our ordinary lives. Both science fiction and fantasy are populated with incidents and problems that the main character has to overcome. These incidents and problems are quite different, usually, from those that the reader has to overcome in his earthly existence.

Fantasy doesn't usually deal with creatures from other planets or with space travel. Fantasy does deal with ghosts, vampires, werewolves, demons, witches, sorcerers, elves, leprechauns, dwarves, fairies, beasts, charms, changes, chants, spells, curses, devils, and talking animals. And none of these is ever explained! The young reader is simply asked (or it's implicit) to accept that these things actually exist. It's very simple: in a fantasy, a young person is asked to *fantasize.*

In most fantasies, the events are set out in a very detailed fantasy world. Sometimes, this world is underground, as in *Alice's Adventures in Wonderland* by Lewis Carroll. Or it may be found inside a wardrobe, as it is in C. S. Lewis's Narnia tales, or even within the microscopic realm inside a human body, as in Madeleine L'Engle's *A Wind Through the Door.* The writer makes no attempt to explain (as he would in science fiction) how this world came into existence. The reader is simply expected to believe that the world of the fairies, for instance, exists. Perhaps it exists in the meadow beyond the reader's house or in the forest down the road, or perhaps it exists in a faraway country; but it exists and the reader must believe that it exists. If the reader does believe, then the fantasy is successful. Details can build credibility. For instance, in the first of C. S. Lewis's Narnia books, *The Lion, the Witch and the Wardrobe,* who would ever question that the parlor of Mr. Tumnus (who is a faun) did indeed exist and that Lucy did have tea there:

THE FANTASY SHORT STORY

Lucy thought she had never been in a nicer place. It was a little, dry, clean cave of reddish stone with a carpet on the floor and two little chairs . . . and a table and a dresser and a mantelpiece over the fire and above that a picture of an old Faun with a grey beard.

Fantasies can be set in early history, when great rulers believed in magic rather than in scientific explanation.

Fantasies can be set in the distant future, and you don't have to explain the miracles that take place. If you do, remember, then you have crossed over into science fiction.

Fantasy for the most part is shrouded in mystery, and these mysteries are never explained, either. In fact, it's this mystery that often attracts the reader. Some people don't like to have mysteries explained. They want to think the events around them happen because there are people with mystical powers. Once these events are explained scientifically, this mysticism is destroyed for the reader. Some people actually feel protected by the mysteries.

I firmly believe that fantasies are good for children, especially for helping to develop creative minds. Children need fantasies.

A beginning writer must realize that in writing fantasy, however, he hasn't been given license to have his main character do and say anything that comes to mind. A fantasy should be logical within a previously worked out framework. The main character should never simply be able to call upon his magical or mystical powers unless you've already provided for that within the framework of the story. You must be fair with your young readers, even though you're writing fantasy and asking them to dispense with disbelief. Even though your main character will be able to do a lot of magical things, if he's all-powerful, all-knowing, capable of getting out of any predicament without any problems whatsoever, then you've destroyed the suspense of the story. Nobody will want to read a story when there's an unsympathetic character, and there'll be no sympathy for the main character if he can get out of any predicament without any problems whatsoever.

Fantasies can be divided into the following types of stories:

1. The Friendly Ghost Story.   Young people love stories about friendly ghosts and other nonhuman characters who live in haunted houses with secret panels and hidden staircases. These nonhuman characters can be historical ghosts who haunt an old house that a family has just moved into or the spirit of a young person who can't rest until a wrong is righted. It's important to remember that in this type of story, the nonhuman characters must never *terrify* the reader, they may only scare him.

Even though friendly-ghost stories have been done again and again, young people still enjoy them. It'll simply be up to you, the writer, to take these old favorites and give them a new twist. Use your imagination to add something different so that an editor will want to buy your story.

The reading levels for these types of stories range from preschool through intermediate. Once a young person has reached the young-adult level, his interest in nonhuman characters often turns to dark fantasy.

2. The Dark Fantasy Story.   Dark fantasy is an extremely popular type of fantasy, especially with young adults. Stephen King's *Carrie* and *Christine* and Ray Bradbury's *Something Wicked This Way Comes* are examples of dark fantasies that appeal to young people, because they have teenage protagonists caught up in the world of the supernatural. This is the fantasy of bad ghosts, vampires, Frankenstein-like monsters, people coming back from the dead, zombies, and, in general, very ghastly and ghoulish characters. These are the characters of some very scary, very bloody, and very gory stories for young adults.

Dark fantasy is also a good place for me to digress for a moment. I hope you're not saying as you're reading this discussion of dark fantasy that this is terrible and that I shouldn't even be discussing stories such as these. I'm discussing this type of story because dark fantasy sells—and it sells very well. Of course, what you write is your own business, and if you're not interested in writing dark fantasy, then nobody's going to force you to. But if you're a serious writer, you should be interested in learning about what interests young people, and one of the things that interests them is dark fantasy.

One of the differences between dark fantasy and a lot of the other types of fantasy is that dark fantasy usually takes place in contemporary settings. You can't tell the setting of a dark fantasy from your everyday existence. (For me, this is one of the attractions.) Dark fantasy can also take place in recognizable historical settings, but the most popular dark fantasies for young people take place in contemporary settings, where the supernatural elements contrast nicely and more believably with what's an otherwise common background. It's this otherwise common setting contrasted with the horrors of demonic invasion that terrifies and fascinates the readers of dark fantasy. The terror comes from knowing that unlike the heroes of fantasies, in which magic spells and miracles are commonplace, the main character of a dark fantasy could possibly die or go mad. This is what keeps the reader on the edge of his seat.

One of the main requirements of a dark fantasy is that the main character put himself in a position where he has found out something he isn't supposed to know and that he'll probably die because of it. If it's not the main character who finds this out, then it's somebody very close to the main character. Some very gruesome things do take place in dark fantasy stories, yet this is seemingly one of the attractions of these types of stories for the young.

I don't believe that dark fantasy affects the psyche of young people as some educators and parents believe. Just how long has it been since you read one of the stories of the Brothers Grimm? Can you remember how absolutely gruesome some of these stories really are? If you can't, then let me tell you that they are! The characters do terrible things to little children in these stories, yet I devoured them as a child, and I've read them to my own children. They can be scary, but they're fun, too, because it's fun to be frightened. My children love these stories, and I do, too! Still! If you try to tell me that these stories will affect me and my children adversely, then we'll . . . we'll . . . cast a magic spell on you!

Dark fantasies are stories of children being possessed by

the devil. They're stories of attempted exorcism. They're stories of young women giving birth to the child of the devil and of the things that subsequently come to pass. They're stories of flesh-eating zombies and of people coming back from the dead to wreak havoc.

The characters in dark fantasy stories often die hideous deaths, and these deaths give the reader the thrill of the horror he's seeking. This, however, is one of the most difficult problems for the writer of this type of fantasy. Since there are supposed to be a lot of horrible things that take place in these stories, you have to decide if you're going to show these deaths on stage or off. Should the death be explicitly detailed or should it be merely hinted at? My suggestion is that you use the device that you think best makes your story an example of dark fantasy and worry about editorial changes later. If you worry about editorial changes before you've finished your story, you might seriously damage it. Don't be afraid to write what you want to write and to put into your story what you want to put into it. If you do this, then you'll write your best story. And after you've written your best story, then you and your editor can make any changes that either or both of you think will make it better and more acceptable. Always leave it to your editor to suggest changes. Don't try to outguess the editor and edit your story first—you may end up taking out some things that you really wanted to leave in but thought the editor would want taken out.

If you're writing dark fantasy, then you'll probably select a nonhuman character to serve as your antagonist. That nonhuman character can be a vampire, a werewolf, a demon, a ghost, a ghoul, or a zombie, or it can be a creature of your own creation. It's important to remember, however, that the traditional nonhuman antagonists may be more real and scarier to your young readers because they already associate certain terrors with these characters; you can take advantage of this association that's already in their minds.

Whichever type of nonhuman character you select, you must be as conscientious in your development of it as you would be with a human character. If the character has been created by you, then you'll have a greater choice of what you can do with it. If

86

however, you're using one of the traditional nonhuman characters, then you'll probably need to do a lot of research to see exactly
how this character has behaved over the centuries. You won't
want to have your werewolf behaving too much unlike the werewolves of legends, unless, of course, you're setting your reader up
for a drastic change in werewolf behavior patterns; but even then,
it should be something that would still be acceptable to all those
werewolf fans out there who'll be reading your story. The same
holds true for your ghosts and your vampires and all your other
nonhuman antagonists. There are certain behavior patterns for all
these nonhuman characters, and your story, to succeed, must find
new behavior twists within these accepted parameters of behavior.

How, then, do you find out how these nonhuman characters should behave? The library is an excellent place to start. There
are always lots of books on myths, the occult, and black magic in libraries, since these are subjects that a lot of people are interested
in. Besides these nonfiction books, you can read other novels and
stories of vampires and werewolves and ghosts and witches and
devils to see how other writers have handled their nonhuman antagonists.

If, for instance, you have a vampire in your story, you'll
need to know that vampires:

a. come out only at night because they hate the sunlight
(You would, too, if it could kill you!),

b. can be killed only by having a wooden stake driven
through their heart,

c. are repelled by crucifixes,

d. can be warded off by garlic,

plus all sorts of other details that can be gleaned from books on the
occult, black magic, witchcraft, and demonology.

One of the most important things you must remember in
dark fantasy is that even if your main character isn't killed off at the
end of your story, you must make sure that there's still a sense of
evil and that it's only a matter of time before the nonhuman char-

acter regroups his forces and strikes again. Everything must *not* be all right at the end of a dark fantasy story. It is very important that there be a sense of foreboding. In this way, the reader is satisfied that the young hero has overcome the evil forces for the moment but knows that it's only a matter of time before the return of the terror and that his victory won't be a lasting one. It's this lingering uneasiness that gives the young reader of dark fantasy the final chill he expects to receive in this category.

You may be wondering just what would motivate your main character to get involved with such inherently evil characters. In one instance, the main character may have been possessed against his will for the sins of his parents, so he would have had no say in his involvement with the evil forces; in another instance, in order to become friends with a certain person, he may get involved with someone who practices the black arts, as in Peter Straub's *Shadowland;* in still another instance, like the Sorcerer's Apprentice, the main character could simply be curious, after reading a book about the black arts, to see what happens if he tries magic for himself. Or the main character may feel that his life isn't quite right and that the only solution to righting it is through an encounter with demonic powers.

It's important to remember that the antagonist in a dark fantasy story must be very evil. Everything he's involved with should be connected in some way with death or eternal damnation. He's motivated by things that normal human beings can't always fully understand— and by a supernatural thirst for blood.

Dark fantasy stories aren't always pleasant for a lot of people, and, in fact, are damned quite frequently by many groups as having a very negative effect on the lives of young people. I suppose that anything carried to the extreme could have an adverse effect, but that's beyond the scope of this book. Often an attraction to subjects that we adults might consider harmful or unacceptable is simply an intellectual exercise for a young person. (During one period in my life, I was extremely interested in finding out more about witchcraft and demonology.) Frankly, it's quite healthy to be inquisitive. No parent should immediately dispatch his child to a psychiatrist at the first sign of interest in black magic.

3. The Sword-and-Sorcery Story.   Young people today are very familiar with sword-and-sorcery characters because
so many of these characters are turning up on television and in toy
stores. They know all about Robert E. Howard's Conan and the
television superheroes He-Man and She-Ra, Princess of Power.
Young people never seem to tire of these heroes, who have been
commanded by kings and queens or sorcerers to search out evil
enemies or to find lost or stolen treasures or magic potions.

In order to carry out the wishes of the person who's commanded him to do these deeds, the hero of a sword-and-sorcery
story often engages in a very long journey, encountering along the
way evil villains, horrible beasts, and magic spells of all kinds.

This particular type of fantasy takes its name from what actually happens in the story. The main character is nearly always involved in clashes in which he must use his sword, usually a magic
sword, and must contend with evil magical spells cast on him by
evil magicians.

Almost all of these characters have incredible physiques.
They come very close to being supermen and superwomen. They
slay dragons, every imaginable kind of prehistoric reptile, and
must pit their wit and intelligence against evil kings and queens
and sorcerers.

The most important element of this type of fantasy is action. A story contains one action-packed battle after another, and
the main character never seems to suffer from battle fatigue. Pac-
ing is extremely important, too, in sword-and-sorcery stories. It
should be fast and furious; it must never let up for a minute, or the
reader will be instantly bored.

In a sword-and-sorcery story, the basic plot has the hero
receiving a command from the good king to go and rescue a stolen
treasure from the evil king in a kingdom beyond the mountains.
The hero accepts the command. When he reaches the border of
the evil king's territory, after numerous encounters with prehistoric
beasts while crossing the mountains, the hero receives a supernatural warning, which tells him that he should return at once to his
home or suffer a terrible fate. Naturally, the hero won't turn back,
being the kind of superhuman being he is, so he ignores the warn-

ing and enters the kingdom of the evil king. When the evil king (or perhaps the evil sorcerer) dispatches his legion of evil soldiers to kill the hero, they're locked in furious battle before the hero and his good soldiers finally kill off the evil king's evil soldiers, take the treasure, and return home triumphantly.

4. Talking-Animal Stories. So often, when people who are interested in writing for young people say they want to write fantasy, they're talking about writing talking-animal stories. Many, many beginning writers want to write in this category. And there's a market for them, despite what you may hear otherwise. Once, when asked whether or not he'd be interested in buying a talking-animal story, a popular editor of children's books thought for a minute, then replied, "Well, it depends on what the animals have to say!" And frankly, I think this applies to all talking-animal stories.

Generally, though, talking-animal stories, besides having animals that talk, teach a simple lesson. All you have to do is remember the talking-animal stories you grew up with: *The Three Bears, The Three Little Pigs, Henny Penny.* These are talking-animal stories that teach simple lessons, but they're successful not because they teach lessons, but because they're fun to read. Young people have enjoyed them for many years.

5. The Enchantment Story. Almost all countries have their legends of fairies and little people who create mischief. These are stories of enchantment, and as such, they aren't violent like the sword-and-sorcery or dark fantasy stories. There's only mischievousness and perhaps some implied violence, which is definitely offstage. There are kings and queens and princes and princesses. There are fairies and elves and leprechauns. J. R. R. Tolkien's *The Hobbit,* an epic fantasy, is an enchantment story. Many people feel that children shouldn't read stories of enchantment because they don't portray the world the way it really is. I beg to differ with these people. There's nothing wrong with stories of enchantment. In fact, I feel sorry for a child who didn't grow up on fairy tales and dream of one day entering an enchanted land. I

90

firmly believe that stories of enchantment are necessary to a young person's healthy mental development. Bruno Bettelheim, a child psychologist, has written an influential book, *The Uses of Enchantment,* which is founded on this very principle.

6. The Walter Mitty Story. Walter Mitty, of course, is the character created by James Thurber. Walter Mitty spent his life daydreaming about all the wonderful things that could happen to him. A Walter Mitty fantasy is a story in which the main character lives a fantasy existence within what is an otherwise normal society. The main character of this type of fantasy could be an elementary, middle-school, or high school weakling who fantasizes that he overcomes the school bullies and becomes the strongest person in school. In addition, he becomes the hero of the football team and gets all the girls. If there's no scientific explanation as to how this has happened (and here that would be very difficult to do), then the story would be classified as a fantasy.

7. The Everybody-Is-Crazy-but-the-Kids Story. This is my favorite type of fantasy; I've used it in a couple of books and a number of stories. In this type of fantasy, relatively normal (well, perhaps a *little* kooky) kids are thrust into a situation where all the adults act strange and the job of the kids is to cope. Young people already think that adults are strange anyway, and these fantasies only serve to prove their point. One plot I've used for this type of story concerns a group of girls from an all-girls' school who go to an inn for the summer to put on a cabaret act, hoping they'll be seen by a Broadway producer; instead, they end up searching for a character called Mr. Spaghetti Man. These stories become almost slapstick in their episodes, but slapstick *is* fantasy, a series of comic events that we'd sometimes like to be involved in if we thought we could get away with them.

Here's a story by one of America's best-known writers of fantasy. I'd like for you to read Jane Yolen's "The Tower Bird." Then I'll analyze it in light of what I've just discussed.

The Tower Bird

BY JANE YOLEN

There was once a king who sat all alone in the top of a high tower room. He saw no one all day long except a tiny golden finch who brought him nuts and seeds and berries out of which the king made a thin, bitter wine.

What magic had brought him to the room, what binding curse kept him there, the king did not know. The curving walls of the tower room, the hard-backed throne, the corbeled window, and the bird were all he knew.

He thought he remembered a time when he had ruled a mighty kingdom; when men had fought at his bidding and women came at his call. Past battles, past loves, were played again and again in his dreams. He found scars on his arms and legs and back to prove them. But his memory had no real door to them, just as the tower room had no real door, only a thin line filled in with bricks.

Each morning the king went to the window that stood head-high in the wall. The window was too small for anything but his voice. He called out, his words spattering into the wind:

> *Little bird, little bird,*
> *Come to my hand,*
> *Sing me of my kingdom,*
> *Tell me of my land.*

A sudden whirring in the air, and the bird was there, perched on the stone sill.

"O King," the bird began, for it was always formal in its address. "O King, what would you know?"

"Is the land green or sere?" asked the king.

The bird put its head to one side as if considering. It opened its

92

broad little beak several times before answering. "It is in its proper season."

Color suffused the king's face. He was angry with the evasion. He stuttered his second question. "Is . . . is the kingdom at peace or is it at war?" he asked.

"The worm is in the apple," replied the bird, "but the apple is not yet plucked."

The king clutched the arms of his throne. Every day his questions met with the same kinds of answers. Either this was all a test or a jest, or dreaming, or an enchantment too complex for his understanding.

"One more question, O King," said the finch. Under its golden breast a tiny pulse quickened.

The king opened his mouth to speak. "Is . . . is . . ." No more words came out. He felt something cracking inside as if, with his heart, his whole world were breaking.

The little bird watched a fissure open beneath the king's throne. It grew wider, quickly including the king himself. Without a sound, the king and throne cracked into two uneven pieces. The king was torn between his legs and across the right side of his face. From within the broken parts a smell of soured wine arose.

The bird flew down. It pulled a single white hair from the king's mustache, hovered a moment, then winged out of the window. Round and round the kingdom it flew, looking for a place to nest, a place to build another tower and lay another egg. Perhaps the king that grew from the next egg would be a more solid piece of work.

Jane Yolen's "The Tower Bird" is a very good example of an enchantment story. It has a king and a castle and a talking bird

We are immediately asked to suspend disbelief, because we have to accept the fact that this king sits alone in his high tower and sees no one at all except the tiny bird that brings him nuts and seeds and berries.

We do learn at the end of the story how the king came to be, but it's a fantasy explanation, not a scientific one. What's not explained (and shouldn't be) is how a king and a tower could be hatched from a bird's egg.

We have sympathy for this king who doesn't know why he's where he is. Yet our final sympathy must lie with the little tower bird, who knows you've got to keep trying, if you're to achieve perfection—in this case, the creation of a perfect king for the kingdom below.

Jane Yolen herself has written, "While realistic fiction deals with small truths, fantasy by its very removal from reality can deal with Truth with a capital 'T.' " So it is with "The Tower Bird."

7

The Historical Short Story

One of the most disturbing things in modern education in the United States is the lack of emphasis on the study of history. Of course, I'm biased. I love history, and I love historical stories. But many editors seem convinced that young people today simply won't read historical stories, so consequently they don't buy many of them for their magazines. Editors want stories of the here and now. Still, some historical stories do slip through, and you can always hope, if you're particularly interested in writing stories set in the past, that your story will be good enough to convince an editor that if it's published it'll be read.

A good story to study is "Amelia and the Bear" by Nelda Johnson Liebig. It's based on an actual letter that Ms. Liebig found in *History of Door County, Wisconsin, Together with the Biographies of Nearly Seven Hundred Families.* In the story, Amelia kills a bear and saves the family pig. It's a fine example of truth into fiction.

In those schools that still teach history, a change is taking place, however. There's less of an emphasis on dates and events than there is on a consideration of the reasons our forefathers did what they did.

There are so many good stories in the history of America. There are also good stories in the histories of other countries, but you're taking even more of a chance of getting a rejection slip if you try to set your story somewhere else besides the United States. There are only a few other countries which you might successfully use as setting for your historical story. England, Canada, and Mexico are among the acceptable countries. Once in a while, stories set in other countries will sell. I remember several years ago reading a two-part historical story set in Australia. I know the editor thought it was excellent. I don't know what the readership of the magazine thought, although the younger the readership, the more likely the story will find acceptance.

Historical stories can bring alive the history of a country. They can show young Americans how and help them understand why the United States came to be as great as it is. A good example is "A Horse in the House" by Lee Wyndham, the story of Temperance Wick, whose bravery has become part of the folklore of the American Revolution. When I was growing up, I distinctly remember reading nothing in the sixth grade but biographies of great Americans. The books were all bright orange. I read every one I could get my hands on. The worlds of these great Americans came alive for me. This is perhaps the greatest challenge of the writer of historical stories: to make history come alive. Young people today are often amazed that young people of yesterday faced many of the same problems that they themselves face. I really believe in the old adage that we can learn from history.

I'm separating western stories from historical stories because, even though the western period is a very important part of our history, it's such a developed category that it seems to deserve this separation. A historical story, then, for our purposes, will be any story set in the past (with the exception of the period covered by the western story) and not obviously belonging to another category, that is, historical mystery, medieval fantasy, etc.

Often, young people think that a historical story will be about only battles and presidents. They never think these stories can be about doctors and writers and artists and businessmen. Historical stories can show vividly, for example, how certain medical advances came about and what the world was like before different types of medicines were discovered or invented. Young people can learn how certain great books came to be written. They can learn how certain machines were invented—machines that, for instance, made it easier to produce different types of textiles.

In order to make historical stories work for young readers, it's important that the writer help the young person of today identify with the young person of yesterday. Even though the clothes and the houses may have been different, all young people have shared throughout history many of the same desires to succeed in their world, to do well in school, or perhaps even to go to school. Young people have always had a difficult time understanding their parents, wondering why they do what they do. Young people of today are sometimes surprised that the problems they have with their parents are the same problems that young people of yesterday had with their parents. Young people of today are also surprised that young people of yesterday worried about their relationships with their friends and about being popular and unpopular. In historical stories, you can show young people how problems similar to theirs were solved in the past. Young people of today will often find that many of the old values remain the same.

But I'm not suggesting that we live in the past. Our attitudes toward each other are changing, fortunately; this is reflected in our history texts, and one of these days it will be reflected in our historical stories. Young people today are no longer portrayed in what used to be their traditional roles. Boys no longer are the only breadwinners of a family and girls no longer dream only of staying home and taking care of the children. Boys are going into professions that at one time only women occupied, and girls are going into professions that at one time were occupied only by men. Our daily lives are different today. We must understand life today in order to understand life as it was yesterday.

One problem, however, with this new awareness is that it has begun to affect stories written about how life used to be. So often this problem affects stories about race relations in the past and stories about the role of women in society.

I get very nervous when there are complaints from certain ethnic groups about how they're presented in historical stories. Historical stories should be written to represent things the way they *were,* not the way certain groups wish they *had been.* We cannot and should not rewrite history, and we cannot and should not misrepresent history to young people—a charge we often level against totalitarian regimes. In fact, it's this truthful representation of history that helps our young people see why change was needed. If we paint things as having been perfect in the area of race relations, for instance, in the past, then our young people will grow up today with the wrong impression of just how much has been gained by many groups in the area of civil rights. Many historical stories involving slaves have been censored and censured by different groups and organizations over the last few years for the way the slaves are portrayed. The writer was only wrong if his portrait was untruthful. What's frightening in most cases is that the writer's portrait *was* truthful. The problem was that these different groups and organizations were upset at the truth.

This same problem often exists in the portrayal of women. Yes, it's a fact that more women are working outside the home today than are not. Modern stories, then, shouldn't portray the woman as mostly staying at home. Conversely, historical stories shouldn't try to convey the impression that women didn't cook for their husbands, wash the clothes, take care of the children, and do all the other chores associated with being a housewife. The bottom line is that the portrayal should be truthful. It should be the way it was, not the way the writer or the writer's audience wishes it had been. Laura Ingalls Wilder's *Little House* series is a good example.

It's very important that you understand that a factual portrayal of the way things were is often a voice against certain injustices of the past (if indeed this is the writer's goal), not a voice condoning certain practices. You must make young people of today

98

understand that it's their right to read in their literature how things actually were in their country many years ago, no matter how unpleasant it actually is to them. There are those who are very keen on making sure that young Germans never forget the Hitler period. We have periods in our own history which we should make sure that our young people never forget, either. You must show young people that they can indeed learn from history.

If you're writing for young people and your story will have a historical setting, there are several things that you should avoid doing.

You need to make sure that you don't make your main character too good to be true. This often happens when a writer is very interested in a historical character. It's often very easy to overlook his bad side. Make him real. Very few of us are good all the time; this holds true for historical characters as well.

In a historical story, it's often very easy to fall into the trap of giving too much background information. Always keep in mind that you'll need only enough background to set up the story. Your young reader will want to get into the life of the main character as soon as possible. Give as much of the background as you can indirectly, that is, through the mouth of the main character.

Make sure your young main character is really a *young* character and not an adult trying to be a young character—unless, of course, you're using an older protagonist.

Make sure, too, that you really want to write a short story for young people, not one for adults. Sometimes a writer really wants to write a story for adults, but writes it for young people instead, thinking that it'll be easier. A young reader will see immediately that your main character is not really young, but is an adult in a young person's clothes.

Don't make your main character too serious. Young people aren't serious all the time; nor were historical young people.

Don't be boring. Make sure you're writing a story and not simply a historical document.

Don't refer to so many historical figures in your story that your reader will get confused by the constant explanations you've had to include.

Make sure your historical references are accurate.

Make sure the dialogue of your characters sounds like young people talking and not like a history teacher giving a lecture.

In writing historical stories, as with writing any story, you certainly have to keep the audience in mind. Very young children require a very simple story, while older readers require a story with a lot of action and believable characters.

Certainly, you can set your story in almost any period of history and in almost any country, but I believe you'll have the most luck if you set your story in the United States during the American Revolution or the Civil War. These seem to be two periods that young people like to read about. (Keep in mind that the western story has its own category and that World War II is covered in the suspense/adventure category.)

The period of the American Revolution still fascinates young readers, mostly because they still read Esther Forbes's *Johnny Tremain*. The Civil War is still being debated in many parts of this country, so it also holds a great deal of interest. Too, many young people are very familiar with Stephen Crane's *The Red Badge of Courage*. These two historical periods still have enough left in them that they can become the setting of very exciting (and very publishable) short stories for young people.

You should remember, too, that American Revolution and Civil War stories don't have to be war stories in the sense of being populated with soldiers and battles. You could simply place your characters in one of these two periods of history. Of course, there would probably be references to the wars, but there wouldn't necessarily have to be any battle scenes.

You must always remember that there's no substitute for a good story, no matter where it's set. You want to make your readers feel that they're actually with your young revolutionary war hero as he moves silently through the dark streets of Boston, going to a secret meeting; or with your young revolutionary war heroine, whose life has been changed drastically, because her family's loyalties have been split; or with your young Confederate or Union hero, as he secretly crosses enemy terrain at night; or with your young Confederate or Union heroine, as she pines for a young man who's been killed in battle.

In writing historical fiction for young people, chronological order is preferable to having flashbacks or changes in the point-of-view. The latter two devices can be extremely confusing, especially in the limited length that you have to work with in short stories.

The historical short story is one of the categories in which an adult as the main character is quite acceptable. This is because often one of the reasons for writing the historical story is for a study of a historical figure. One of the ways of handling the point-of-view is to have the main character seen through the eyes of a young person, or, especially for younger readers, through the eyes of a talking animal. This type of story is usually about how the great historical figure came to do whatever it is he's famous for. Often, the narrator, the young person or the talking animal, gives the impression that he had a lot to do with the famous historical figure's becoming famous! A very good example of this is *Ben and Me* by Robert Lawson. The book is subtitled "An Astonishing Life of Benjamin Franklin by His Good Mouse Amos, Discovered, Edited & Illustrated by Robert Lawson." I'll talk more about point-of-view in Chapter Sixteen.

Whenever you're deciding on a historical event to weave a story around, you should first make sure that the story either is or can be made exciting. It must be a story in which somebody overcomes a problem. Only in this way can there be a conflict to resolve.

If you're choosing a historical subject for very young people, then it would be very helpful if you chose an object that they're familiar with. Who invented television, for instance, or the radio or the electric light bulb or the automobile or the telephone? They're certainly familiar with these inventions. They would be interested in finding out more about the inventor and what life was like before these inventions were around.

Older readers will read stories of people whose names are unfamiliar to them as long as it's somebody who's accomplished something that's important to them. They may, for instance, be interested in who invented computers, video games, a myriad of other technological marvels that have been invented in their lifetime or before they were born, without which they feel they simply can't survive. Sports figures, too, are always good subjects for biographical short stories, as are musicians and movie stars.

Stories of local historical interest can usually find a market in local newspapers or regional magazines, although stories written for a younger audience will find limited acceptance. Stories of local interest will find a greater audience if they have national appeal.

Once you've decided in which period of history you want to set your story, then you'll need to do some research. This is one category in which research is extremely important. But there's scarcely a period in history that hasn't at least been covered by one book or by several articles, and they should be your starting point for your historical short story.

You'll need to avoid getting bogged down in too much historical research. It just isn't needed for short stories. You'll need only enough to be accurate and to set the mood for the story. Often, suggestions of historical information are better than paragraphs of long historical narration. I'll talk more about research in Chapter Thirteen.

It's also very important for you to remember that young people reading historical short stories will accept as fact what they're reading. You must therefore never fictionalize factual information. No one will really know whether your characters did or didn't say what you have them say, but you should keep all the actual historical facts accurate. Your job is to bring the facts alive, not to rewrite history.

8

The Western Short Story

As I've indicated, I'm separating the western short story from the other historical short stories because of the special place that the western occupies in the minds of most Americans.

Most young people look upon the Old West as something nostalgic and romantic—a view they probably got from their parents. In fact, many young people in the eastern part of the United States still believe that much of the West is populated by cowboys and Indians. Actually, it still is. They may not do all of the same things that they used to, but it's very easy to see the Old West come alive here in Oklahoma, for instance, with the rodeos and the Indian powwows. In my particular area of the state alone, the Kiowa, the Apache, and the Comanche have their own tribal headquarters where they hold their powwows, in which they do their traditional tribal dances in full-dress. Geronimo, the famous Apache chief, is buried not far from where I'm writing this.

There was once a time when television had several weekly western series. These programs are still being shown on many independent stations. Young people of today still have the western story available to them, and many of them still watch these programs, although I don't think the western story has as much appeal now as it did several years ago. I'm sure this will change. There'll come a time, probably in the not too distant future, when westerns again will be essential television fare and consequently, western stories will be sought after.

For many writers, however, the thought of writing a western story is just not very appealing. Many writers, frankly, think that western stories are for the uneducated masses, not at all for the sophisticated, and that they are just a waste of good writing time. If you feel this way, then you probably haven't read many westerns. There's a great literature in the field of westerns. I always tell my students that they should never criticize a category until they've mastered it. In one of the writing courses I teach, I always insist that my students write at least one short story for each of the categories I'm discussing in this book. They seem to resist westerns more than any other category. Yet often when they've finished the course, they're proudest of their western stories.

A western story probably will paint good and evil more clearly than any of the other category stories, as can often be seen when the good guys wear the white hats and the bad guys wear the black hats. If you're being honest with your readers, however, you'll see that it's very difficult to remain 100 percent good or bad in the world we live in. As your western story develops, your reader should see that the good guys don't seem as good and the bad guys don't seem as bad as they did in the beginning. One of the reasons this is true is that all western stories must be set between the years 1865 and 1899, that short span of time that was actually the Old West. This was a time when there was either very little organized law enforcement or what there was was largely corrupt, often almost as corrupt as the outlaws these officials were sworn to defend the West's citizenry against. This was a time when very wealthy men owned large ranches and to keep out competition either bought out, forced out, or killed off their competitors. Whole towns were often run by either one man or one company.

In such a setting, anybody willing to stand up against such odds was immediately elevated to the role of a hero. This man could rob a bank, steal from cargo trains, rustle cattle, and be labeled both an outlaw and a hero to some people, because he was thumbing his nose at this corrupt authority.

The western is another category in which people try to rewrite history, when what they should be doing is telling what actually happened. There were people who went to church on Sunday then robbed trains during the week, for example, because they thought they were standing up for their rights in doing so. You do want to be careful when writing your stories, however, so that you don't seem to be promoting such behavior. You must make sure that the characters against whom such crimes were committed fall into the same category as did King John in the Robin Hood legend. Most people think of Robin Hood's having lived in a time when it really was permissible to rob from the rich and give to the poor, because that was the only way the poor had of making sure they survived. They were without the laws we have today, which ensure for the most part that these things don't happen. You must make sure that in your story the message comes across that the people did these things because there really were no laws and that the lawmen were often corrupt. You must make sure that your young readers read your story as history and not as a blueprint for present-day behavior.

There are several different types of western stories that you can use as the basis for your story.

1. The Lawman Story.   In this story, your main character is either a sheriff, a marshal, or a deputy, and his life is usually seen through the viewpoint of his son or daughter (although in western stories, as in some of the other categories, you don't always have to have a young protagonist).

In the lawman story, the lawman is pitted against an outlaw. He's motivated by his sense of duty to the people of the town as well as by some other reason. In order for the story to be well balanced, the lawman should be motivated by some other reason than fighting the outlaw. The outlaw could have killed the mother and father of a young friend. The outlaw could have been responsible for inciting a party of renegade Indians to raid a homestead where children lived. The outlaw could even be a relative of the sheriff. There are many reasons that the main character would want to apprehend the outlaw other than the fact that it's the job he's paid to do. Whatever reason you choose, it balances your story and makes it much more interesting.

2. The Outlaw Story. This is the opposite of the lawman story. Generally, the outlaw story will succeed only if the person becomes an outlaw because he's wrongly accused of a crime and has to flee. A young person, for instance, could have been wrongly accused of a crime, fled the area, then decided several years later to return and clear his name.

Very seldom is murder one of the reasons the person is considered an outlaw; however, his having been *falsely* accused of murder is acceptable, as is his having killed a person in self-defense, especially if a member of his family had been killed (either on purpose or accidentally) by an unscrupulous lawman. The person could also have been swindled out of some money and have stolen it back, only to be branded an outlaw. In the end, wrongs are usually righted. If the main character has been living a life of crime, then he's reformed, the reader realizing that this would never have happened if the first unfortunate and unfair event had not taken place.

3. The Cattle-Range Story. This type of story lends itself to having a young main character. It is usually set on a ranch or on a long cattle drive, which could involve young people. These are stories about cattlemen battling farmers, sheepherders, droughts, cattle rustlers, and unscrupulous bankers, as well as all of the other problems that people trying to start a living on a ranch would have experienced during the Old West. The sons and daughters of your main adult character could help their parents on the ranch or the farm and even be the focal point of the story.

106

4. The How-the-West-Was-Won Story.   This is also an excellent type of story in which to have a young person as the main character, for these stories deal with treks across the continent in wagon trains, the construction of railroads, stagecoach lines, pony express routes, telephone and telegraph line construction, and many other things that helped to open the West to the rest of the United States. Your young main character could be the only man in the family, for instance, because his father was killed either by disease, Indians, or outlaw raiding parties. Or he might have run away from home and gotten a job working to build the railroad. He would, of course, experience all kinds of hardships. A young girl, too, could be thrust into immediate adulthood, if her mother died in childbirth. The young girl would then become responsible for taking care of her father and her brand-new sibling, probably at the expense of having a life of her own.

5. The Cavalry-and-Indian Story.   This is probably the most changed type of story in the western category, because of our new awareness of the equality and treatment of various ethnic groups. No longer is the Indian automatically cast as the savage and portrayed unsympathetically in a western story. He's sometimes the protagonist while members of the United States Cavalry are the antagonists. But this should never stop you from writing a story that does have Indians as antagonists. There were bad Indians, just as there were bad white men.

It wasn't at all unusual for young people to live on cavalry posts out West, so it would be very easy for you to have a young main character in this type of story. Often, these young people were the children of the men stationed at the fort or the orphaned children of settlers who had lived in the area and been massacred. The children had to suffer the same hardships as the adults, so it would be very easy to tell of hardships from their point-of-view.

This type of story also offers you the opportunity to tell a story from the point-of-view of a young Indian boy or girl, giving your young readers what would probably be a totally different perspective as to what life was like in the Old West. "The Leaf Painter" by David Hoxworth, a short story that tells the Indian legend of how the leaves came to be so brilliantly colored in the fall, is one of the best examples of stories using this point-of-view.

6. The Stranger-Who-Rides-into-Town Story.   In this type of story, a stranger rides into a town that is having trouble. The stranger is usually not known to anybody in the town, but he's discovered to be exceptionally skilled at doing something—usually something pertaining to guns. The people in the town recognize that the stranger is special and have respect for him, but they don't completely accept him. There are outlaws in the town who are creating problems. Nobody in the town is strong enough to do anything about these problems. The townspeople see that the stranger and the outlaws keep clear of each other, not out of fear, but almost out of mutual respect for each other. Even when the outlaws continue to threaten the town, the stranger stays clear, because it's not his fight. Eventually, though, the outlaws threaten someone close to the stranger, who fights the outlaws and wins. The town is now safe. The stranger is accepted.

If this plot sounds familiar, it's because you've seen it in hundreds of western movies. It's one of the standard plots. A version of it appeared in Jack Schaefer's book *Shane* and the movie based on it, in which a young boy is important as a viewpoint character. It also makes an excellent basis for a western short story. The stranger can, for instance, start working for a widow who has a young girl or boy. The woman needs a husband and the girl or boy needs a father. The stranger wants a wife and child. They all realize the others' needs, but it takes a threat against the woman or the child by the outlaws to make the stranger act. When he does, the man, the woman, and the child are brought together. This story could easily be handled from the viewpoint of the young person.

If you're interested in writing western stories, then you're probably already familiar with a lot of westerns. I don't think this is a category that usually attracts the unfamiliar immediately. If you aren't familiar with this category (and even if you are), there are several areas that you need to pay very close attention to, because readers of westerns know quite a lot about the Old West, and you want to make them feel that you do, too.

You need to know how young people dressed. There are certain fabrics today that weren't available then.

You need to be aware of the customs of that period. Some things that young people do today weren't acceptable then.

You need to know what a young person was expected to do on a day-to-day basis. What time did he get up? What time did his chores begin? Did he go to school? For how long during the day and for how many years?

What kind of food did young people eat?

How did young people talk? The language of the Old West was full of words peculiar to the period, and you need to be aware of this. You can find examples of western language in other western stories and in books about the Old West. A number of lists of words used in the Old West have been published over the years. *Ramon F. Adams' Western Words: A Dictionary of the American West,* the University of Oklahoma Press, is the best source.

Research is very important in writing western stories, as you can see. For instance, if you're writing a story about *wagon trains,* then you'll need to know that the *wagonmaster* would often yell, *"Yoke up!,"* which meant that the oxen would have to be harnessed (if oxen were being used instead of horses), and then *"Stretch out! Stretch out!,"* which meant that the train was supposed to uncircle from the night's encampment. Once the wagon train was on its way, it's important to know which trail it followed and what the particular problems of that trail were. Was it the *Santa Fe Trail,* or the *Overland Trail* or the *Cimarron Trail?* Once the wagon train was on the trail, then the *bullwhacker* would make sure that the oxen kept going.

Probably more than anything else, if you're writing a western story, you should know what kinds of guns were available to the person who lived in the 1865-1899 period. This is almost a fetish with readers of westerns, even young readers. If you make a mistake—if you describe the gun wrong, or if you use a gun that wasn't available during this time, for instance—then you'll be caught in the error and your editor will hear about it. Then you'll hear about it, and that might be the end of your western short story writing career!

9

The Romance Short Story

If you visit a bookstore that carries young-adult romances, you'll notice that many of these books carry a picture (usually a photograph) of a teenage boy and girl, looking lovingly at each other over a soda. This is a very good indication that the story within is what the publishing industry considers a *sweet* story, as opposed to a *sensual* story. And sweet stories are usually the kind that you'll be writing if you're interested in writing romance short stories for young people.

      The young-adult romance story is a relatively new form of the romance category. These stories are usually concerned with first love problems and with growing up. They're generally written for the eleven- to fourteen-year-old girl, but more and more of the stories are being written today to attract boys. These stories are mostly about boy-girl relationships. They're considered very ten der stories, with nothing rough in them. They're also considered very sensitive. Any expressions of physical love are kept to shy kisses, handholding, and gazing into each other's eyes. Here's an example from "Blind Date," a short story by Nan Friedlander:

> I looked down and saw that her face was streaked with tears. Her pleated skirt was smudged with grime from the clay court. Something got to me then. All of a sudden she wasn't so darn perfect any more. She was human after all. I rubbed my cheek against that soft hair, and I think I felt her press her head closer against my shoulder. Probably I imagined it.

These stories are simply written. The style is clear. The sentences and the paragraphs are quite short. It's important to remember that a lot of dialogue is needed in young adult romance stories. Here's how Lexie and Ted discuss tennis in "Blind Date":

> "Where do you play?" I decided that she'd recharged her batteries by now.
> "Glenbrook Park."
> "On weekends, I guess, huh?"
> "Yes, and at other times. The courts are lighted till 10:00 p.m."
> "Say, why don't we play sometime? How about next Saturday?" Out of the corner of my eye, I saw Ted wink at Sally.
> "If you like. I'll meet you there at 7:30."
> "Isn't that your dinner hour?" I didn't want her to faint on me.
> "I mean 7:30 a.m. If you don't get there early, you have to wait for a court. I don't have time to do that."

Young adult romance stories are written about the problems that concern teenagers every day. This is often the downfall of beginning writers. You'll often overlook as trivial something that the teenager considers a matter of life and death. If you're to be a successful writer of young-adult romance stories, then you must be able to zero in on what really matters to teenagers and weave your story around these things. One of the subjects you might consider is the confusion that comes about when a teenager realizes for the first time that he's in love. Another subject could be the confusion that results when a teenager starts trying to determine exactly who he is and what his place in society is. Still other subjects might be gleaned from the struggles that a teenager encounters as he begins to mature. In Jeanette Mines Ryan's *Reckless,* for instance, fourteen-year-old Jeannie Tanger discovers the bittersweet pain of first love when her romance with school troublemaker Sam Bensen alienates her from her friends and family. In Tina Sunshine's *An X-Rated Romance,* Emily and Sara, two thirteen-year-olds, fall helplessly in love with Mr. Garfield, their blue-eyed eighth grade English teacher and concoct a zany plan to seduce him.

The heroines in these stories are usually sixteen, and the heroes are usually between seventeen and eighteen. The reader, as I mentioned, is much younger. This is important: young people who read these stories are seeking answers to their problems from *older teenagers.* They'll not read about younger people, and they prefer not to read about people their own age, thinking that people their own age just simply aren't mature enough to have solutions to *their* problems.

I honestly think that this is a very difficult category to write in if you don't have a good rapport with today's teenagers. If every time you see a group of teenagers you begin to think less-than-kind thoughts, then perhaps you shouldn't consider writing young-adult romance stories.

One thing you absolutely must avoid when writing young-adult romance stories is a nostalgia trip. You won't be successful with your stories if you write about the prom you attended when you were a teenager ten, twenty, or even thirty years ago. I hate to tell you this, because no matter how much fun you had and how you think it would be so wonderful if teenagers today had that much good, clean fun, you simply won't find an audience for your story. Today's teenagers aren't interested in what teenagers of yesterday did (unless your story is clearly labeled a "time travel" story!). They might feign some interest in what their parents did as teenagers, but they won't at all be interested in what a total stranger did. The world of the teenager is very small. The center of the universe is himself. This universe is the space between home and school and maybe the beach, the local shopping mall, or wherever it is that he and his friends happen to hang out. There are a few other planets, his friends, orbiting around him.

If you don't know any teenagers, you need to meet some, and you'd better be prepared for a trip into another world. You need to talk to them and you need to listen to them. This is very important if you're planning to write about them. You simply can't write in this category in a vacuum. You must be very sensitive to the problems of today's teenagers. It won't hurt if you've had a course in adolescent psychology—at least this would give you some help in understanding why teenagers do some of the things they do.

You can't go into this category thinking that everything a teenager does is crazy. Teenagers are very complex creatures, and their behavior, which to some observers may seem irrational and bizarre, is very complex, full of definite rules and regulations.

What types of characters will you choose for your young-adult romance stories? Most guidelines from magazines reveal the necessary information. The girl should be about fifteen or sixteen, and she's definitely a virgin. It doesn't matter how many dates she's had before your story; your story is the one in which she really finds her first love. The boy she's in love with is between seventeen and eighteen; he isn't necessarily a virgin, but if he's not, it isn't flaunted. In any case, the boy whom the girl is falling in love with has too much respect for her to sleep with her.

The story should also have the accepted stock characters, those characters readers have come to expect in a young-adult romance story. There should be the best friend. There can also be an understanding adult, but *never* a parent, since most young people are convinced that their parents just simply don't understand them! And there's usually a jealous ex-girlfriend or ex-boyfriend. Almost all writer's guidelines will tell you the same information. Don't try to change anything, especially if you're a beginning writer. The editor expects this because the readers expect it.

No matter how much various groups cry out against this, the heroine of a young-adult romance story is generally very attractive, although she often doesn't see herself as being attractive. There's a physical attraction to the boy in the story, but this isn't the primary attraction. She's also attracted to his inner qualities—his warmth, his sense of humor, his sincerity—and sometimes to his family. She respects him, too, and this is the primary attraction.

There must always be an obstacle to overcome in the relationship. Often, the boy isn't immediately interested in the girl. He may be more interested in playing sports, in cars, or in a number of other things that teenage boys are interested in. Sometimes the girl thinks the boy is interested in another girl, someone she considers flashier than she is, someone who, although she has only heard talk, *may not be a virgin!* This is a source of great anguish to her. It's at this point where it even enters her mind to give up her virginity in order to keep the boy, although the hero (and this is very important) has never asked her to do so. The best friend or the understanding adult will tell her not to do that, but she herself must be the one who makes the final decision. In the end, all the misunderstandings that have marred the relationship are solved, and the boy and girl are together.

The geographical setting of a young-adult romance story isn't usually as exotic as the setting of an adult romance. Most of these stories are usually set at home or school. Sometimes they're also set in places where teenagers hang out, like shopping malls or at the beach or in the mountains. Some stories can also be set in a town distant from where the main character lives, especially if the heroine is going to visit a relative. She could then meet a boy and carry on a correspondence with him after she returns home.

It's best to avoid setting a young-adult romance in a large city, such as New York or San Francisco. These settings tend to overwhelm the stories and often end up dominating them. Most settings of young-adult romance stories are in small towns, recognizable to almost any young person anywhere. Even young people who live in large cities will be able to relate to these small towns as being similar to their neighborhoods, but the reverse never seems to work. If the story has a less-than-accessible setting, then it should be something familiar like a beach, which, although available only to a small section of the country, is a setting that teenagers throughout the country recognize and relate to because of television and motion pictures. A beach, therefore, isn't an alien environment, even to someone in Kansas. The secret to choosing a setting, then, is to choose an environment that's not alien to teenagers even though it may not be accessible to a large number of them.

Once in a while, young-adult romance stories can be set in foreign countries where the heroine is on vacation. This setting can be used to further the action of a story and to provide the challenges and complications that the main character must face in order to mature, as in the case of the young heroes of "Rescue from Hungary" (pages 59-66) and "Escape from East Berlin" (pages 178-182), who have to demonstrate courage and cooperation to come safely out of the foreign dangers. But you must remember that a geographical setting should be developed to the point that the details you include help clarify or point up the central theme of your story or somehow intensify the action. Always keep in mind that the readers of young adult romances (as well as readers of the other categories) have grown up on almost a steady diet of television and they're used to stories that move along at breakneck speed. (I'm not concerned in this book about what you think of feeding them more of the same. I'm concerned about your selling your stories.) It's very important that you remember this if you're thinking about including *anything* in your story that'll slow down the action. Detailed descriptions of settings will definitely slow down the action if these descriptions aren't central to the story. The teenage reader for the most part has a shorter attention span than most adults. He expects a fast-paced story, in which action and dialogue are the most important elements. He'll not tolerate your wonderful reminiscences of last year's trip to Greece.

There are also some young-adult romance stories that can be set against a *professional* background, in which the main character works after school. This can often be a job that the main character hopes to continue with after he graduates from high school. Today, such jobs are in grocery stores, in stores, in shopping malls,

115

or in fast-food restaurants. One reason these professional settings are so good is that they offer the opportunity for the main character to mature by supplying major challenges in his life. There could be a time when the main character is scheduled to work but has been asked to a big dance by the hero of the football team. There could be a situation in which the main character has a boyfriend who's in debt and she's left alone with a cash register full of money. There are many possible story lines with many possible challenges in a professional setting. Good examples of this are Helen Wells' series about Cherry Ames, who eventually became a nurse; and of course, the series of novels about "Young Doctor Kildare" by Max Brand, the basis of many movies and a television series.

If you're familiar with the adult romances being written today, you know that some of them have very explicit sexual scenes. You'll not find these in stories written for young adults. The main characters in young-adult romance stories don't actually make love to each other. The sexual scenes are much more discreet and less passionate when it comes to expressions of physical love.

One of the reasons sex is avoided is that the most passionate (and this is relative, anyway) scenes come at the end of the story, so that anything beyond *this* takes place offstage and is left up to the imagination of the reader. So often, the heroine has been kissed only once before in the story by the hero and the last sweet and tender scene comes right at the end as there's a fade out. It's in these last few paragraphs that the hero and the heroine admit their love for each other, embrace in a tender kiss, and the story comes to an end. You should always remember that in a young-adult romance, physical passion is secondary to emotional complications.

The emotional and physical needs of young people aren't the easiest things to write about, but they're sometimes the easiest things for young people to *read* about. Writing young-adult romance stories is difficult because when we write about the emotions and physical needs of other people, we often sound silly or puritanical or staid or anything but natural. And another thing, when we're writing about emotional and physical needs, we reveal a lot of things about ourselves that we didn't know before.

I've been discussing romance stories geared to young

adults because the greater part of the market is for them, but romance actually enters the picture much earlier.

For first through third graders, love stories are usually about getting married and having babies. Of course, this same theme can be the theme for stories geared toward older readers, but these stories are then fleshed out by more expressive feelings.

Romance stories for the younger ages are usually filled with teasing between the sexes, giggling, note passing, harmless flirting, and strolls down the halls of the school for the purpose of looking at each other.

Although romance short stories are usually geared toward girls, more and more stories are being geared toward boys, using boys as main characters. Thank goodness editors are realizing that there really are a lot of young boys who can use the emotional uplift from reading the same type of story that young girls have been reading for years. Harry Mazer's *I Love You, Stupid!* is a good example. It's about seventeen-year-old Marcus Rosenbloom, an aspiring writer, who has only one problem: he's still a virgin. In his efforts to "become a man," he learns that neither sex nor love is ever simple.

Of all the readers of young-adult romances, the readership the stories appeal to the most is twelve-year-old girls, because they are at the beginning of puberty. There's probably no other time in a girl's life when romantic fantasy is so important. This is an extremely difficult period for her. She has entered what will be the loneliest time of her life. She's becoming very interested in boys, but the boys aren't interested in her. Her life is suddenly very frustrating and she doesn't know what to do about it. She is, as a matter of course, driven into a romantic fantasy world because this is the only place where her dreams can come true. She has many crushes on many boys, and they come to nothing because these boys are still interested in playing sports or games or (and this is very difficult for the twelve-year-old girl to understand) each other (and I don't mean sexually).

Out of this frustration, the twelve-year-old girl starts looking to junior high boys—or more likely to singers and actors on television or in the movies. She thinks about boys constantly. She mopes around the house. She makes life difficult for others because life is difficult for her. The lucky girl will find some outlet in what she reads, and whether her parents (or you) like it or not, some of the more explicitly written stories for young people have probably kept many twelve-year-old girls out of psychiatrists' offices.

What these twelve-year-old girls don't realize is that even if the boys in their school classes paid attention to them, they'd never measure up to the girls' standards. No one can satisfy those lonely feelings that keep emerging all the time. The twelve-year-old girl would still be driven into her romantic fantasies of that great love who'll come to sweep away her loneliness and take her away forever. In your young-adult romance short stories, it's important that you accept this behavior as the norm.

Twelve-year-old girls are able to suffer and endure, and although they might never admit it, there's a certain pleasure in this suffering. They can live with the painful yet truthful lyrics of the songs they listen to endlessly on the radio. They know that just around the corner will be the right boy for them. The only problem with this is that so very often the young girl never thinks of herself as the perfect mate for this perfect boy. Nothing's ever right about her. Her hair is the wrong color. Her complexion is terrible. Her ears stick out too much. Her nose is crooked. So are her teeth. She weighs too much. And on and on and on. To everyone else, especially to her parents, she may be beautiful, but to herself, she's ugly. She has created for herself the perfect boy, but she thinks of herself as less than perfect. No wonder she suffers so much!

It's important that you understand how young girls think they'll meet the right boy, for this will be an important part of your story.

Many young girls believe in love at first sight. They believe that they'll simply bump into the right boy and that things will be perfect. Many young girls simplify romance into (1) love at first sight, (2) a kiss, (3) marriage, and (4) children. They always meet the person they're going to marry by chance. They're never introduced by anybody else. This is the recurring romantic fantasy of all young girls. In Dian Curtis Regan's delightful *I've Got Your Num-*

ber, a wrong telephone number for Emily Crocker turns into an unexpected introduction to Austin Brandt, a college man who sounded terrific on the phone and was even more gorgeous in person!

Boys are still viewed by most young girls as the superior animal, even though in more and more young-adult romance stories, equality of the sexes is playing an important role. There are many groups that don't like the idea of showing the man as the superior animal in any story, especially the romance story, but it's a matter of fact that young girls do feel this way. Some editors will buy stories in which the girl seems as strong emotionally (and perhaps physically) as the boy or in which a boy is attracted to a girl because of her dominant characteristics, such as self-assurance, and because she seems to have none of the characteristics associated with pubescent girls. But, frankly, I think you're taking a big chance of having your story rejected if you don't follow most of the traditional patterns.

For most readers of young-adult romance stories, the end of the story, whether it takes place on stage or (more likely) off-stage, is marriage. And there's never any hint that the marriage will be anything less than perfect. But young girls today have varying opinions of the roles of husbands and wives. Once they've gone through the rather traditional male-dominating-female courtship, what happens after marriage is quite a different matter. It's almost as though the young girl reader expects a complete transformation. I've seen this rather unfortunate set of circumstances in real life. The young girl falls head over heels in love with a young boy. The girl is a good student and makes very good grades. She could possibly win a number of scholarships to a lot of top universities. Her parents don't understand why she's so infatuated with this young man (even though they have nothing against him personally), because the young girl has a chance to go far in almost any profession she might choose. The young boy, on the other hand, likes the attention he's getting from the young girl. It makes him feel secure in his manhood. The young boy and young girl plan to get married. Here's where most young-adult romance stories end, with plans for the wedding. The stories in the mind of the young girl reader, however, don't end here. In her continuing fantasy, the young boy and young girl do get married and go away to college. The young girl becomes a nuclear physicist and the young boy becomes a football coach, professions they both want to follow. (The most incredible romantic fantasies take place in the minds of the young girl reader after she's finished reading a romance short story.) Of course, this is where some of the problems in real life start. It's fortunate that most twelve-year-old girls do grow out of their romantic fantasies and become realistic. There are some, however, who retain these fantasies into their marriages and either endure miserable existences the rest of their lives or file for divorce.

Still, romantic fantasies are very important to young people, just as fantasies of all kinds are important throughout our lives As I've indicated, fantasies can often be carried too far, but they can often help get us through what would otherwise be very difficult times, and there's absolutely nothing wrong with that. We all fantasize, and there must be a reason that we do. I think this is why: if it weren't for her romantic fantasies, the twelve-year-old girl would have a much more difficult time getting through life than she does. And so would all the rest of us.

One thing I've noticed is that young girls of today are much more in touch with their romantic fantasies than were young girls of even just a few years ago. The fantasies are much closer to the surface, and young girls of today find them less embarrassing to reveal to others than did their counterparts of the past.

It's important to remember, however, that what's romantic to one person isn't necessarily romantic to another. There are, of course, some old standbys that just never seem to fail us in this area. A moonlight swim, for instance, or a long walk along a beach, holding hands, with a stop from time to time for a gentle kiss—these activities still conjure up romance for most people. Or a candlelight dinner, or standing in front of your door after your first date, facing each other, wondering if this'll be your first kiss. Or sitting together in a darkened movie theater while your date is whispering sweet nothings into your ear, his arm around your shoulders. Some things just never change.

10

The Religious Short Story

One of the best markets for writers of young people's short stories is the religious field. In fact, most of the publications for young people listed in *Writer's Market* are published by religious denominations. And more and more of these publications seem to appear all the time. If there's one drawback to these markets, though, it's that they don't pay very much, but you've heard it before and I'll tell you again: As a beginning writer, making a lot of money shouldn't be your primary concern. Your primary concern should be getting published. You need to be building your track record, and writing religious short stories is a good place to start.

There's a tremendous demand for writers in this area, because so many of the publications appear weekly and each publication is written for a specific age rather than an age group.

But, again, this is definitely another one of the categories that's difficult to write for, if you're not familiar with the religious teachings of a particular religion or denomination within a religion. There are some nondenominational markets, but these are still *religious* markets, and at least some understanding of the religious teachings espoused by the publication is necessary.

As with the other categories, it's important to study the markets for religious short stories. Often, people interested in writing religious short stories write for their particular denomination, although this is not the case for the publications that are nondenominational. You need to study the markets *carefully*. You can find the addresses of religious publications for young people in *Writer's Market*. Write for a copy of their publications. Look at the kinds of stories they're publishing. Go to the library and read some of the books for young people written by people from the different denominations. Watch some of the religious programming on television. Talk to various church leaders. Doing these things can help you zero in on what might make an excellent short story for publication in a religious magazine.

There are several types of religious stories.

1. Stories Based on the Main Books of the World's Religions.   The main books of the world's great religions are:

a. Buddhism
    1. The Dhamma/Dharma
    2. The Sangha

b. Catholicism, the Catholic Bible

c. Hinduism (Sanskrit sources)
    1. The *Ṛg-veda*
    2. The *Atharva-veda*
    3. The *Śatapatha-Brāhmana*
    4. The *Upaniṣads*
    5. The *Gṛhya-Sūtras*
    6. The *Dharma-Sūtras*
    7. The *Manu-Smṛti*
    8. The *Bhagavad-gītā*
    9. The *Mahā-Bhārata*

10. The *Rāmāyaṇa*
11. The *Purāṇas*
12. The *Tantras*
13. Kālidāsa
14. Bhartṛhari
15. Bhavabhūti
16. Rāmānuja
17. The *Gīta-govinda*
18. The *Sarva-darśana-saṃgraha* of Mādhava
19. The *Adhyātma-Rāmāyaṇa*

d. Islam, the Koran

e. Judaism, the Torah

f. Protestantism, the Protestant Bibles, the Book of Mormon

These are the authorities in the different religions, but the language is often too difficult for young people to understand. Stories based on the actual teachings of these books make excellent introductions to the books themselves, so that as the young person gets older, he's better able to understand what he's reading.

These stories, then, would actually be retellings of the major events from these sacred books. They should adhere strictly to the teachings of the prophets and the other major characters. A well-written story based on the sacred books of a particular religion will always find a market.

2. Stories Fictionalized from the Main Books of the World's Religions. Some stories, rather than adhering strictly to the sacred books of a religion, are simply based on information found within. In these kinds of stories, fictional characters are often added to make the story more interesting or more detailed. In this way, you're able to use dialogue, description, and action that doesn't actually occur in the account in the sacred book.

Here's an example of fictionalized dialogue from Nancy Castle's "Jeremiah Becomes Unpopular" which was *based on* Jeremiah 26 and was written for third and fourth graders in Southern Baptist Sunday Schools:

123

"Stand in the courtyard of the Temple and speak to the people who have come to worship," God told Jeremiah. "Tell them everything I tell you. Don't leave anything out. Maybe the people will listen and turn from their evil ways.

"Tell them," God continued, "that if they do not listen and obey the laws, I will destroy the Temple. And the name of Jerusalem will be a curse word among all nations."

There's really nothing wrong with fictionalizing material from the sacred books, because doing so often gives the story more life and make it more appealing to young readers. But you must remember that the basic story mustn't be changed.

Some religious publishing houses won't be interested in these fictionalized accounts based on the sacred books, because they believe that the truths of the sacred books have been disturbed. These are usually the publishing houses connected with more fundamentalist denominations, which adhere to a very strict interpretation of the sacred books. But other religious publishing houses, those connected with the more liberal denominations, will accept these stories fictionalized from the sacred books as long as they don't conflict with the basic teachings.

One of the problems you'll encounter in fictionalizing stories from the sacred books is determining just how much fiction you want to inject into the story. It's often difficult to know how much will be too much. You must remember that you're not trying to confuse your young reader with what the teachings of the sacred book actually say; you're trying to make the teachings clearer. Teachers and parents often complain that they many times have to *unteach* information published in fictionalized stories based on the sacred books.

If you're in doubt as to some of the elements in a religious short story that you've written because you don't belong to the particular denomination for which it was written, then have someone in that denomination read it to see if you're distorting the actual teachings. If you are, perhaps they can suggest changes, so that when it reaches the editor's desk, it won't be rejected because of the false or distorted religious information in it.

3. The Story Based on Religious Concepts and Principles. These stories, rather than being based on the actual sacred books, are based on concepts and principles that have been developed from the sacred books, principles by which members of the various religions conduct their everyday lives. Stories can often be based on the questions that children ask about their religions. Who is God? Who is Allah? Who is Buddha? Questions similar to these. These are questions that we adults seldom have quick answers to. They're sometimes abstract questions, questions that we think we have the answers to, but when pressed, seldom do. In trying to verbalize answers to young people's questions, we often seek out help from stories that attempt to explain these abstract concepts in simple terms.

If you're writing stories based on these religious concepts and principles, then it's very important that the language you use be simple. This frees the young person (and the adult) to grasp the difficult concepts. Analogies work very well in these stories, but you need to make sure that you understand analogy and use one that works well as an explanation. This type of story will, of course, require that you read and understand the more difficult interpretations of the concept before you can write about them simply. But a good source of information and help will be children themselves. Often they've already worked out the concept in their minds and their explanations are as clear as a bell. With minds uncluttered, they've been able to clarify a very complicated concept in uncomplicated terms. If you're lucky enough to have a young person invite you into his world, you will have a valuable head start in helping you incorporate, using simpler language, an abstract concept into your religious short story.

4. The Fiction Story. One of the growing areas in religious short stories for young people is the story that is purely fiction. This type of story is wide open as to what kind you want it to be, that is, mystery, suspense/adventure, romance, fantasy, science fiction, or western. All of these categories could also become religious short stories, even though this is one of the types of religious stories in which religion doesn't have to be mentioned. If the story is interesting, with lots of action and interesting characters, with young people solving their problems in a realistic manner within an acceptable environment, then there's a very good chance that your story will be accepted for publication. The characters must be excellent role models for the young readers of the particular publication. It really doesn't matter if the story presented has a religious theme, as long as it presents positive moral values.

If you want to include religious elements in your story, then these elements should be an integral part of the story. Tacking on a religious note as an afterthought is a common downfall of beginning writers.

Keep in mind, too, that religious information shouldn't be preachy. Young people don't like to be told what they have to believe; they like to discover for themselves.

5. The Seasonal Short Story.   Seasonal short stories may be your best entrance into the market for religious short stories. Some of the seasons, ceremonies, and holidays of the major religions are:

a. Buddhism
    1. Vesākha/Vaiśākha-pūjā, for remembering the birth of Buddha.
    2. thūpa/stūpa-pūjā, for remembering Buddha's demise.

b. Catholicism
    1. Christmas, for remembering the birth of Christ.
    2. Easter, for remembering the death and Resurrection of Christ.

c. Hinduism
    1. Dīvālī, the Festival of Lights.
    2. Holi, the Spring Festival in honor of Kṛṣṇa.

d. Islam
    1. The Friday prayer
    2. *zahat,* the duty of paying legal alms.
    3. The *ramadan,* a fast that lasts a lunar month.

4. The *haj,* a pilgrimage to Mecca.

e. Judaism
1. Passover, for remembering the miracle of the exodus from Egypt.
2. Shabuoth, for remembering when God revealed himself to Moses and the Jewish people.
3. Sukkoth, for remembering the forty years of wandering by the Jews in the desert.
4. Rosh Hashanah, for remembering that all the world is judged before God's heavenly throne.
5. Yom Kippur, for remembering the Jewish sense of at-homeness with God.

f. Protestantism
1. Christmas, for remembering the birth of Christ.
2. Easter, for remembering the death and Resurrection of Christ.

Although there are relatively few holidays compared to other possible subjects for stories, editors are always looking for stories that tell in a new way about the special celebrations of the world's great religions. It's very important, however, to remember that seasonal stories usually have to be submitted at least six months in advance.

One of the main differences between religious stories and stories for other markets is in the area of audience age groups. Most religious publications are published for single grades rather than for larger-spanning age groups. This means that there will be a need for a lot of stories but that you'll have stricter parameters. You'll need to know, for instance, what a third grader wants to know and how he thinks, and you'll not be able to slip backward toward the second grade or forward toward the fourth grade.

Another thing to remember in writing religious stories is that more and more editors are wanting fewer and fewer obviously didactic stories. Don't think that because you're writing a religious story you have a license to preach. Teri Martin's "Christmas for Joey" is a good example of a short story that presents a religious message without preaching. It's a very poignant story that strikes a good balance between pathos and bathos. Without any reference to biblical passages, it illustrates nicely the Christmas spirit by its central theme of personal sacrifice. Young people, even those from very religious homes, no longer automatically accept being preached to.

When you're developing religious characters, it's important to make them well rounded and normal. They don't need to be bad, but they don't need to be perfect, either. Young readers want to believe that even young people who follow religious teachings have weaknesses. Nothing is more counterproductive in a religious story than to have a central character who's so perfect that nobody could possibly measure up to him.

Religious short stories should basically do the following things:

1. They should help young people develop a strong faith by allowing them to identify with the characters of the sacred books.

2. They should help young people grow naturally into a style of life that will reflect the beliefs of their religion.

3. They should help young people realize that there's often a religious alternative to solving life's everyday problems.

4. They should strengthen the family unit by providing young people with information that will allow them to participate in the worship process.

A lot of editors of religious magazines will look at a story first to see if some part of it will capture the young reader's attention that has nothing to do with religion. They feel that if the young reader can be captured in this way, whatever spiritual message the story contains will be absorbed indirectly. There's nothing wrong with this. Medicine is often sweetened.

11

The Mainstream Short Story

There are basically two kinds of fiction, category and mainstream. Mainstream fiction may be defined as fiction that doesn't fit comfortably into any of the other categories. Because young people compartmentalize and *categorize* more than adults, they seem to enjoy category stories more than mainstream. For many writers and critics, though, mainstream fiction seems to be a few steps above category fiction. Mainstream fiction is usually thought to be concerned primarily with the ideas expressed by the characters, the way the characters say things, depth of characterization, moments in a person's life, thoughts, and philosophies. Often, a mainstream short story can fit into a particular category, such as mystery, but when the writer elevates the characters above the mystery elements of the story—when he makes the words they speak seem to be more important than the action going on around them, when what happens to them as people becomes more interesting than the fact that they've solved a crime (or committed a crime)—then the writer has probably written a mainstream story.

The mainstream story is often merely a moment captured in a person's life. A young person could be looking at a photograph and remembering good times or bad times or sad times. He could be opening a present and be engulfed in a flood of memories. Or he could be at a dance, as in the following short story by Lucille Curtis, wondering what the point of going to a dance is if nobody is going to ask you to dance:

The Dancer

BY LUCILLE CURTIS

Smile. Laugh. Ha-ha. Look interested. Someone will ask me to dance if I look lively and like fun to be near. Of course, it won't be boys who know me, because they probably think I'm dull and boring, but there are one or two strangers here. If someone doesn't ask me to dance soon, I'm never coming to another dumb dance again. Here comes someone. Is he looking at me? Well, he was cute, but obviously taken.

Dancing is good exercise and relieves muscle tension. The movements are based on basic life rhythms. I dance at home to Neil Diamond and Michael Jackson.

What is the point of going to a dance, if you don't dance? Dancing with anyone would be better than standing around watching all these slow dancers wrapped around each other. I am not here to be picked up for a ride, or to stand around the parking lot smoking and whispering. I am not here with my boyfriend so that we can change around with our pairs of friends. I am here with Jan and Carol, who haven't danced either. We have split up so boys won't be intimidated by having to approach three of us—my mother's suggestion. We are here because we hoped that someone exciting—someone different— would show up and in a rosy haze, we would dance.

Let's face it. How many romances actually start at dances? Neil Sedaka could write a sad song with that line. Most of the boys here are in my classes at school. We laugh and joke in Spanish class and chemistry. But this is apparently not going to be the place to meet that certain someone.

Do the unattached seventeen-year-old spinsters plan these dances? Definitely not! If they did, they would match everyone up at the door, whether they liked their partners or not.

And it's not that I don't have other interests—that I'm just hanging around until some guy gives meaning to my life. I sew, I have a lot of homework, I'm on the swim team, and I'm planning to go to college. I watch TV with my folks. Jan and Carol and I go bowling, rollerskating and to movies. But every now and then we get caught by the enticing promise of a school dance, with a local deejay as host. If someone asked me to go steady, I would do it just long enough to come to one of these dances and have someone to dance with.

Oh, oh, here comes Bill Johns. Six inches shorter than I, the screwy brain of the school, with a weird personality. I think he's looking at me. I've got to get out of here. Hurry, out to the drinking fountain in the hall. I'll smile at the boys at the fountain. No, I'm not embarrassed to dance with Billy Johns. In fact, I would dance with anyone, in a flash. I was just afraid that he was going to walk by, without asking me.

"The Dancer" is an excellent example of a mainstream story for young people. If you examine it carefully, you'll see that it doesn't fit comfortably into any category. It could possibly be the *beginning* of a romance story, but it isn't a romance in itself. It is merely a moment captured in the life of a young girl at a dance, but it is a story that reveals very well what many young girls (and young boys, too) have often felt in similar situations. After reading this story, many young people will probably say, "I know *exactly* how she feels!"

The first thing you should keep in mind is that the basic difference between category stories and mainstream stories is that category stories are usually written for entertainment and mainstream stories are usually written to be pondered. If you've something to say that you think is important, in which the action isn't the most important element, in which the theme or the characterization dominates, then you might consider writing a mainstream story.

Another difference between category stories and mainstream stories is seen in the action. Both types can have action, but it's handled differently in each. Writers of mainstream fiction generally try to avoid ordinary action scenes such as car chases, gun battles, or fist fights, but if your mainstream story requires such scenes, then make sure that they're as different as you can possibly make them. In a category story, the action is usually one of the most important elements, often at the expense of other elements in the story. In a mainstream story, the action often takes a back seat to the setting, the characterization, or the theme of the story. If there are action scenes in your mainstream story, make sure that you avoid all clichéd words in describing them.

A mainstream short story needs to touch the hearts and minds of its young readers. It must be complex in its intentions, yet capable of being understood by its audience. It must be ambitious in its handling of the plot, the characters, and the theme. Most mainstream short stories require that you use more complex characterizations and have a rather ambitious theme—sometimes a theme that's controversial.

The plot in a mainstream story is usually a mere skeleton

onto which a writer adds the more important elements of characterization, theme, and symbols, until the story has been constructed. The reader knows the plot is there, but it never gets in the way of the full expression of the more important elements.

The most likely market for a mainstream story would be a slick publication for young people ages 16-18 that uses stories that reproduce some slice-of-life moments.

What you have to remember is that category short stories for young people are much more marketable than mainstream short stories.

Part Three

Putting It All Together

12

Writing Through the Ages . . . from Preschool Through Young Adult

Stories for young people may be divided into different age groups for many different reasons. Most writers will tell you that they write for a particular age group. This is because they feel comfortable with this audience. They've discovered their voice. As a beginning writer, you may not have yet found your voice. You may set out to write for the intermediate group and find that your story is actually a primary story or a young-adult story. Don't despair—go with your voice. Don't try to force what you have to say into another age group if it wasn't meant to be.

The most common divisions of stories for young people are:

1. *Preschool,* ages two to six

2. *Primary,* ages six to eight

3. *Intermediate,* ages eight to twelve

4. *Young adult,* ages twelve to sixteen

But there's a lot of blurring and movement back and forth between the boundaries. Some intermediate readers still read primary stories, because they like them. Other intermediate readers have already crossed over into young-adult stories, just as some young-adult readers have already crossed over into adult stories.

1. Preschool Stories. For the preschool age group, stories can be word-and-concept stories, as well as rewritten nursery rhymes. Many of these stories will be read aloud to members of this age group. Good examples are Dr. Seuss' *Cat in the Hat* and *Horton the Elephant.* Once the story has been read to the child, he'll often go back to it many times on his own, using the pictures to provide the clues to the text of the story as he "reads" it to himself or to his parents.

Often, stories for this audience actually have mostly pictures and very little text on every page. The pictures are supposed to carry fully half of the story, supplying the descriptions and the details of the characters. If your story is accepted by the editor, the editor will arrange for the artwork. This is his business. Unless you're a professional artist, don't send artwork with your story. And please don't make the mistake that a lot of beginning writers make: paying someone to illustrate their story. You're wasting your time and your money, and you'll probably kill all the editor's

137

interest in your story. Especially as a beginning writer, you simply have nothing to say about the artwork.

In writing for preschoolers, it's very important that you repeat the key words and phrases throughout your story. This is a very effective way of getting your story's message across. In *Horton the Elephant,* by Dr. Seuss, Horton's repeated phrase, "I meant what I said and I said what I meant. An elephant's faithful one hundred percent," is a good example of this.

A magazine picture story is probably one of the most difficult types for the novice to market. The text of the picture story must sell itself—it must stand alone. Sometimes I think that one of the reasons new writers spend so much time worrying about illustrations is that they think these illustrations will sell the story for them. This simply isn't the case. If the story can't stand up without the illustrations, then it simply isn't good enough for publication. The pictures might indeed enhance the story, but *enhance* is the key word.

A picture story may be written for several reasons. It may be written to teach a lesson or to present special information. It can be a glimpse of another country or a certain section of the United States. It can show readers history or it can show them some details of something they may already be familiar with, such as a circus, a zoo, a grocery store, or a school. But, above all, it *must* entertain. You have to remember that the main reason young persons will enjoy the story is that it entertains them. Don't ever forget this.

You should also remember that the story must appeal to the adult who's going to read it to the child. A good example is VaDonna Jean Leaf's "Timothy Toad in a Hole," which has some very descriptive language that an adult will enjoy reading and a child will enjoy listening to:

> One wet, wishy, plishy morning Timothy Toad went for a walk in the rain. The mud oozed around his feet and tickled his toes. He hopped and skipped and jumped, and he fell down into a deep, deep hole.

If it doesn't appeal to the adult, then he may skip over your story and read someone else's. You certainly don't want this to happen.

When writing your story, you should keep in mind that with the passing years, values and restrictions have changed. We live in a freer society, in which old barriers and old codes have broken down. You must remember that the children who'll be reading your stories live in a different world from the world we lived in at their age. White children no longer play only with white children; they play with black children and Hispanic children and Oriental children. Boys no longer play just with little cars and girls no longer play just with dolls. Your stories must reflect these changes if they're to find a place in the market.

2. Primary Stories.   Stories for this age group must be simply presented in easy-to-understand language. Stories should have a single idea, and everything that happens should contribute to that idea. Further, a simple plot is required to hold the reader's interest. Stories for this age group usually range from 300 to 500 words in length. Sometimes they can be around 700 words, but almost never contain more than 900.

Some primary stories are for young people who're just learning to read; others are for children in the upper end of this age range, who're not yet comfortable with longer, more difficult reading material. Readers in this age group are interested in almost all of the categories. Some of the stories are written to enable even the youngest reader to read on his own. You must take great care, however, to make sure that these stories don't seem like picture stories. Sue Alexander's wonderful *Witch, Goblin,* and *Ghost* series is a very good example. These stories about three well-loved companions who have all sorts of adventures are written for young people just beginning to read. The simple plots hold the reader's attention from beginning to end.

This group does have its picture stories, but they're produced so that they seem more like illustrated stories than picture stories, that is, where the text is more important than the illustrations. There are also stories in this group that are written for an

139

adult to read to the young person.

Young people in this age group aren't afraid of words, even though many primary stories are graded vocabulary stories. Ungraded stories, or stories with more difficult words, will give the reader in this group the feeling that he's reading a bigger story, since he's forced to look up several of the words in his dictionary. But the graded vocabulary stories in this group often give the young person the feeling that he's a good reader because he doesn't have to look up any words. This can be a very positive reinforcement. If the young person has to look up too many words, then the pleasure can be taken out of the reading, and one thing you should never do is take the pleasure out of reading just for the sake of a few big words.

It's still very important in this age group to make sure that the story interest is high. It's important that you *show* your reader what you want him to know, not just *tell* him. In Gay Seltzer's story "The Zucchini Cat," she doesn't just *tell* the reader that Zucchini the cat is hungry, she *shows* them:

Zucchini's ears were pointing up, and her whiskers were twitching. Slowly a pink tongue crept from the cat's mouth, and small hungry noises shook her furry body.

This is a good example of how an author can keep the story interest high. Ms. Seltzer makes the reader *see* that Zucchini is hungry.

Young people in this age group are very interested in stories that deal realistically with modern young people and their problems. If you've a special feeling for the everyday problems of young people, then this is probably a good level for you. Do make sure, however, that the problems you put in your story are problems that young people in this age group are interested in. Steer clear of your own adult interests.

3. The Intermediate Story. This is a period when young people like to read stories that supplement the information in their school textbooks without seeming to do so. They may want to read a story set in a foreign country. They may want to read a story set in a particular historical period because they've just been studying that period. Teachers push these types of stories, and therefore, editors are receptive to them.

This age group is really fun to write for because the young people in it are interested in reading just about any kind of story. This is the age group I prefer, and it does seem to be the best market for short stories. The young people in this group like to read stories about young people older than they are, or at least the same age. They don't normally read stories with characters who are younger; if a young person happens to be reading such a story and somebody starts making fun of him, he drops the story like a hot potato, even though he was only half finished and was enjoying it very much! This group is *very* impressed by what the older kids at school think about them.

There are still boys in this group who want to read only "boy" stories, and there are still girls who want to read only "girl" stories, but the lines aren't as definite as they used to be, and roles are no longer stereotyped, for the most part. Girls enjoy reading adventure stories, and boys enjoy reading sensitive romance stories. The barriers really are breaking down. Editors, though, are probably breaking them down much faster than are writers.

This whole age group usually wants stories with lots of action and solid stories with uncomplicated plots. But the subject interest is limitless. Stories of yesterday, today, and tomorrow are read avidly, as are grim stories and funny ones. Mysteries, stories about families, sports stories, stories about pollution, stories about space exploration, tales of other people and places—all will find an audience in this group.

Stories for the higher age range in this group should focus on contemporary problems. It would be wise to use both girls and boys in your stories. The writing must be narrated from the point-of-view of the main character—everything should be presented through his eyes, his senses, and his emotions. These stories also should be fast paced. The length of these stories is usually 700 to 2,000 words; 1,500 to 1,800 words is considered the most desirable.

This is also the age for easy-to-read stories, written to interest a fourth or fifth grader, but written with the reading vocabulary of a first or second grader. These stories should be lively, use a lot of humor, and/or include a lot of mystery or suspense/adventure. A good example is Florence Parry Heide and Sylvia Van Clief's *Mystery of the Mummy's Mask.* In this story, readers are immediately caught up in trying to solve the mystery, because the reading *interest* is high; and since the reading *level* is low, they have very few problems getting through the story. These stories aren't easy to write, and many writers have grown gray in the process or given up altogether.

4. The Young-Adult Story.   This is also known as the teenage story, but many of these stories are read by ten- and eleven-year-olds. Today, some writers use both terms to label two different types of stories. Teenage stories seem to be less serious than young-adult stories. I'll use the one term, *young-adult,* to describe stories written for young people in this age group.

This group of readers is usually interested in stories about main characters who have grown up and have finished school. What'll happen to them when they finish school and have started working or are beginning college holds a tremendous interest for the young people in this group.

The girls in this group are very definitely interested in serious romance stories. All the other categories have their audiences, too.

Young adults of today are interested in story themes that were unheard of just a few years ago in young-adult fiction. There are a lot of problem stories written for this age group. Some of the problems young adults are interested in reading about are racial problems, premarital sexual encounters, homosexuality, divorce, alcohol-related problems—almost anything that an *adult* would consider a problem. Stories similar to those written by M. E. Kerr, Judy Blume, Nancy Garden, and Cynthia Voigt are what they're interested in reading. These writers seem to be able to zero in on the parental, religious, sexual, and social questions facing young people today. Look particularly at M. E. Kerr's *Dinky Hocker Shoots Smack!,* a story about a girl who eats too much; Judy

Blume's *Are You There, God? It's Me, Margaret,* a story about a girl approaching adolescence; Nancy Garden's *Peace, O River,* a story about opposition to a nuclear-waste disposal plant; and Cynthia Voigt's *Izzy, Willy Nilly,* a story about a popular and pretty girl who loses her right leg.

Today, the main characters of young-adult stories strive to understand themselves and others, the new morality, politics, and civil disturbances. They struggle with issues such as idealistic new worlds, the raising of the underprivileged to equal status in an egalitarian society, and equal rights for women. The main characters of these stories explore, experiment, and come to grief in much the same way as their real-life counterparts.

Young-adult stories deal with more complicated relationships, values, and feelings. Some romance might be involved, but explicit sex, while acknowledged, is almost always offstage.

Young adults will accept plenty of terror in their stories, but usually not graphic descriptions of gore and violence. They also enjoy stories that delve deeply into the psychological aspects of their existence.

No subject matter is taboo, but good taste is all important, although it often seems that the only difference between a story for a young adult and a story for an adult is the age of the main characters.

Young adults demand all the elements of good fiction—plot, characterization, conflict, complications, suspense, drama, and a satisfying solution. Story background is of great interest, but it should be familiar: school, part-time job, sports, camp life—these are very good.

Some of the magazines for this age group are designed for either boys or girls, but they usually try to please both. You'll have a better chance of selling your story if you have both boys and girls as main characters, even though one or the other will play the leading role. Generally, stories for this age group range from 1,200 words to 3,500 words; 1,600 words to 1,800 words is the preferred length.

In this group, you'll also find high-lo stories, which are written for young adults who are reading below their average reading level. These stories must appear to be the same as those written for the normal reading level, but must be geared two, or sometimes three or four, years below in reading level. These stories are often illustrated with photographs rather than drawings. They're usually contemporary in their settings and packed with fast action, humor, and sometimes romance. The dialogue is short, and the issues discussed are uncomplicated within a strong plot line.

13

Collecting Information and Ideas

Several years ago, when I applied for membership in the Crime Writer's Association of Great Britain, I received a letter from Bonney Harris, then secretary of the association. She had just read my adult short story of South Africa, "I'm Sorry, *Baas*," in *London Mystery Magazine*. In her letter, Mrs. Harris said, "I think you must be South African, since you write so knowledgeably about the country."

Well, I'm not South African. I did spend time in South Africa when I was working on my doctorate at the University of Port Elizabeth, but I was born and bred in Texas, and I now live in Oklahoma. But Mrs. Harris's comment—and she wasn't the first to make it—points up something that's important to all writers: the need to be keen observers of the world around us.

Merely observing is usually not enough, however. You must write down what you observe. And I mean write down every-

145

thing, every day—even things that seem insignificant. Later, a seemingly insignificant detail can add reality to your story.

When I travel, I try to blend in with the people around me. I often pretend that I'm one of the local citizens. I love to get caught up in rush-hour crowds—it makes me feel that I'm doing what the local citizens do every working day of their lives. And I always find something in these crowds that I can use in a story.

I read all the local newspapers. (I never rush out and try to buy a home-town newspaper.) I usually take home at least one copy of a local newspaper or clippings of particular interest. Truly, a newspaper is a gold mine. Suppose you're writing a story set in a small Iowa town. Where else but in the local weekly could you find out what your main character would be doing? One night he'd go to club meetings. Another night he'd go to a school program. Where would he buy his car? His clothes? His food? The local newspaper can give you all this information.

I always watch local television or listen to local radio, just to learn what the people are listening to.

I walk as much as possible when I'm in another city. Walking is the best way to get to know any place you visit.

I shop in the stores where the local citizens shop and seldom where the tourists go. I note the prices of the goods so that I won't have my characters paying too much or too little.

Wherever I go, I listen to people. I don't mean that I go out of my way to eavesdrop. But you're not eavesdropping, are you, if you happen to be sitting in a seat—anywhere—next to where an interesting conversation is unfolding? Some of the best stories are right around us, whether we travel one thousand miles or one block.

I haunt airline offices and travel agencies for timetables and brochures that might help me add reality to my stories. Simply walk into one of their offices and ask them if they would mind if you took one of each of their brochures. They won't mind— they're used to it.

I have a very large collection of maps of cities, states, and countries from all over the world. Many travel clubs give these maps free to members or sell them at a nominal fee. All kinds of maps, too, are available in bookstores. I've often used maps to help me get my characters from one part of a city to another or from one part of a country to another.

Travel guides, too, are extremely helpful. They can often be purchased at the end of a year for much, much less than what they originally cost; naturally, that is when you should buy them. For writing purposes (and often for travel purposes), they are still very much in date, and they're invaluable for helping you put just the right detail into your story.

It's also easy to get telephone directories of the locales you want to use in your stories. I have a library of telephone directories from all over the world, from Las Vegas to London, from San Francisco to Stockholm, from Honolulu to Hong Kong. Once, these directories were free of charge; now, however, they cost a small amount. But it's worth it to have all the information they contain. I can have a character stay at the La Lagon 2 Hotel, Route de la Petite Corniche in Dakar, Sénégal, West Africa (I've never been there). I can have a character eat at Café de Paris, King's Alley, Christiansted, St. Croix, U.S. Virgin Islands (I've never eaten there). All these names and addresses may be found in the local telephone directories.

To show you that I practice what I preach, I want to examine some of my short stories so you can see the types of information I've been able to include in them because I took notes when I traveled.

Several years ago, I spent a week in Windhoek, the capital of South West Africa (Namibia) and, as usual, I kept a very copious record of what I did, the things I saw, the people I met, the places I went. Later, many years later, I incorporated some of this information into a story about South West Africa, entitled "Death in the Caprivi." Here are some of the things from my journal that found their way into the story:

1. . . . the heavy traffic of Kaiserstrasse onto Peter Muller Strasse and headed for the Tintenpalast, the main headquarters of the South West African Administration . . .

147

2. . . . ahead of her she could see the building on a rise overlooking the heart of Windhoek, the capital of South West Africa . . .

3. . . . Windhoek looked . . . like a German city set down in the middle of a desert . . .

4. . . . on a guided tour of the romantic German castles in the Windhoek area . . .

5. . . . amidst the near-desert surroundings of the Windhoek area . . .

From the notebook I kept in N'Djamena, Chad, when I was Fulbright Professor of linguistics at the university, I included the following information in my story, "Escape Across the Chari":

1. . . . the Air Afrique DC-10 from Paris touched down at N'Djamena International Airport at exactly one o'clock in the morning . . .

2. . . . the rebel forces under Colonel . . . may attempt to capture the city at any moment . . .

3. . . . the Chadian officials seemed to be searching everyone thoroughly . . .

4. . . . I've been trying to contact one of the French military doctors all day . . .

5. . . . those fishermen's *pirogues,* the long dug-out canoes they use on the Chari . . .

6. . . . it's moored just below the customshouse . . .

7. . . . then turned into the Rue du Sultan Ourado and drove to the Avenue Général Brosset . . .

8. . . . across the Chari, they could see very few lights in Kousseri. . . .

When I was in South Africa, working on my doctorate, I

never missed a day writing in a notebook about all the things that had happened to me, so I was able in a number of my stories set in South Africa to use these very important details. In "Invasion of Port Elizabeth," I used:

1. . . . arriving in Port Elizabeth to pick up cargo bound for the north of England . . .

2. . . . who wanted to see Port Elizabeth cleared customs, walked up Jetty Street, and lost themselves in the crowds in Main Street . . .

3. . . . at the Hotel Elizabeth, about 20 kilometres from downtown Port Elizabeth . . .

4. . . . off to their hotel, the King Edward, which overlooked Port Elizabeth and Algoa Bay . . .

5. . . . at the hospital in the Kwazakele Township . . .

6. . . . turned the automobile onto N 2, . . . could see the skyline of Port Elizabeth . . .

7. . . . several ships at anchor in Algoa Bay, waiting their turn to dock . . .

8. . . . N 2 became N 15 as they turned northwest toward Uitenhage . . .

Although your travels can be a very important source of information for your short stories, your primary source will probably be the library. There is scarcely a subject that hasn't had several nonfiction books written about it, and these books can help you in your writing. But you shouldn't forget to read fiction, too (and this can be adult fiction). Fiction will give you a feel for time and place that you can't often get from nonfiction books on the same subject.

But if your library doesn't have a book on the subject you're interested in, don't give up. There's probably a magazine article available, and the place to find out about it is in the *Reader's*

Guide to Periodical Literature, which indexes articles by subject and author. This will probably be your best source for the most up-to-date information on a subject.

The *National Geographic Magazine* is also a gold mine of information on people and places. It has helped me on many occasions to give just the right flavor to my stories.

But don't forget the best resource of all: your librarian. Librarians are in libraries to help you! Having been a college professor for over twenty years, I often think that I know everything there is to know about a library; still, I seem to learn a new source of information every time I talk to a librarian.

You do need to be cautioned about one thing, however. In doing research for a story, it's often very easy to become so interested in a subject that you'll extract a lot more absolutely fascinating information than you'll need. This is normal, and it's fine—as long as you don't include all of this information in your story. You must always remember that no matter how interesting the material is, if it bogs down the narrative of your story, it should be omitted. Using unnecessary, irrelevant information seems to be a problem especially of beginning writers of historical and science fiction stories.

As a beginning writer, you should realize that you're not expected to know everything. You do, in fact, often have to do a lot of research. But remember, research isn't the only way that you can collect information and ideas. One of the most important ways is simply to keep your eyes and ears open.

14

Mastering Editorial Requirements

What do editors want? Well, according to some of my editor friends, it depends on the time of day, or whether or not they've had their morning coffee, or whether they've just been chewed out by the editorial director, or many, many other things that may cause you to gasp. You may be wondering how in the world you'll ever be able to publish a short story if this is what you're going to have to deal with. Actually, what it should help you realize is that editors are human, a condition that very few writers ever even consider attributing to them. Editors often don't really know what they want, even though they'll send you nicely printed editorial guidelines for their magazines. What you should always remember, though, is that editors know exactly what they want when they see it!

Many editors will tell you that they want stories in American settings about today's young people who are able to solve problems suitable to their years. That's true. But for a number of years, I had young characters in foreign settings who often solved problems no adult could have solved. The point here is that almost anything you write that's within the bounds of good taste is marketable *as long as you find the right market for it*. My stories fit perfectly the magazines they were published in. In fact, many of them were developed specifically for certain magazines. I once had an editor ask me to change the setting of a series from America to France, because he thought the main character of the series (who was absolutely brilliant!) would be more acceptable as a French girl than as an American girl. It was his opinion that American young people don't accept *brilliant* American young people as readily as they accept brilliant foreign young people.

Often editors will tell you they want fresh ideas or fresh approaches to old ideas. The readers of the magazines change, but not the age the magazine is written for; that means that each magazine will continue to be written for a certain age group but that the members of that age group will constantly change. The age groups are always concerned with the same developmental information, which means that the magazine must deal with the same information over and over. This is a very difficult situation for a magazine to be in. The editors don't want to reprint the same stories year after year after year, even though they have a new audience almost every year. They want new stories about the same information. This, then, is your job as a writer: to write a story with a fresh approach to an old idea.

Editors are also on the lookout for current themes that the writer can treat realistically. But don't confuse current with faddish or popular: I'd never suggest that you write a story on anything popular or faddish unless an editor has specifically requested you to do so. If you do do this, chances are by the time your story gets to an editor, it'll be out of date. There's less of a problem with this in writing short stories than in writing books, but you're still taking a chance that you'll be wasting your time.

If the subject you want to write on is controversial, write on it. Don't try to outguess an editor. Don't waste your time wondering if it'll be rejected. Write the story, send it out, and if it comes back, then send it out again. If it's a good, well-written story, it'll probably eventually find a home, because there really are editors out there willing to take chances—almost to lay their jobs on the line—for a story they think should be published.

Editors usually like stories that are interesting to read, fun to read, exciting to read—anything except what they've just read that they don't like! You may be wondering how you're supposed to know what it is that they've just read. You can't know this, of course. You're just supposed to write the best possible story you can write and then send it out. If you're lucky, it'll get into the hands of "your" editor right away. If you're unlucky, then you might have to wait a while to be published. But there are some guidelines you can follow that will help you get published sooner.

In order to master editorial requirements, you must have an understanding of:

1. Categories of stories

2. Age groups, reading levels, and story lengths

3. Point-of-view

4 English grammar and usage

You've already been given the information concerning the categories of stories in chapters Three through Ten; and the age groups, reading levels, and story lengths in Chapter Twelve. Point-of-view will be covered in Chapter Sixteen. I just want to mention here that a sound knowledge of English grammar and usage is also absolutely essential to your being able to write well. Specifically, understanding syntax, the formation of sentences, can have a decided effect on your ability to make your writing flow smoothly. You need to know, in other words, how to *manipulate* your sentences.

While magazines come and go, most editorial requirements stay basically the same. Of course, they may from time to time move from magazine to magazine. I'd now like to look at some editorial requirements as they exist for short stories in publications for young people. I have purposely *not* listed the names of the publications, because, as I've said, the publications may come and go, but the requirements remain basically the same. If you can master these editorial requirements, then you can use them for any publication they happen to fit at the moment you're seeking a home for your short story.

In *Writer's Market,* you'll find the editorial requirements for young people's publications that accept short stories. You need to pay very close attention to these requirements. You may be able to change some of them later on, but certainly not until you've sold the publication a number of stories and the editors know you well. Don't tamper with the requirements in your first short story.

Here are some samples of editorial requirements that you might encounter and some ways I think you should go about mastering them:

1. Stories and articles must have a Christian frame-of-reference. This means that the stories this publication will accept must entertain first and foremost but be set in a home, a church, or a camp where Christian religious teachings are a part of everyday life. You may not even have to mention religion in your story, but ideals of religious training must be adhered to. These stories may usually be in almost any category.

2. All stories published are geared toward entertaining the reader. Humor is probably tops here. But exciting, action-filled stories would also have a place. Serious themes and well-developed characters would probably be wasted.

3. Adventure, nature. No science fiction, talking animals, or religious stories. These people are interested only in realistic stories, preferably stories set in the great outdoors. Animals in these stories would probably be welcomed, but stories featuring them should be about the finding of a hurt animal or about how man and animals co-exist in the environment. The feeling that all the beauty in nature is created by a supreme being would be accepted, too, but this should come through indirectly, not from something that anybody would say directly.

154

4. Short stories for beginning readers. Humorous stories, holiday themes. Almost any category of story for beginning readers (refer to Chapter Twelve) will be considered, but the special needs are for humorous stories and for holiday themes. You need to remember, too, that there's at least a six-month lead for holiday stories. If you're not familiar with the vocabulary of beginning readers, do some research before you start writing.

5. Honesty; selflessness; bravery; adventure; true or true-to-life stories; stories that portray problems encountered by the use of drugs, alcohol, or tobacco; and stories related to parent-child and boy-girl relationships. Within the confines of good taste (and I know this is relative), this publication will accept very straightforward stories about problems that confront America's young people. You'll find no dodging of issues here.

6. Parables that are written in modern style and that teach Christian principles. In order to write for this publication, you must have a very secure knowledge of the parables of the Bible and the ability to translate the parables into modern terms.

7. Authentic historical and biographical fiction, adventure, retold legends relating to monthly themes. The first thing you'd want to do here is to get a copy of the monthly themes, which the editors have probably developed more than a year ahead. Stories for this publication would have to be thoroughly researched, because you would be teaching as well as entertaining, but the entertainment element would probably be what would sell the story to the editor.

8. Realistic, historic, fantasy, science fiction, folk tales, fairy tales, legends, myths, picture stories. Be careful. Any publication that would list all these areas would probably demand the highest of professional standards. Why? Because many of these are areas that beginning writers want to write in and in which they very often produce a lot of unpublishable material. Make sure that you're quite familiar with all the classic fairy tales in order to know what the masters have written and in order to make sure that you aren't retelling badly someone else's tale. A course in mythology probably wouldn't hurt, either.

9. *Fast-moving stories that appeal to a boy's sense of adventure and/or sense of humor. Avoid preachiness, simplistic answers, and long dialogue.* It's best to be familiar with what young boys are doing today before you attempt to write for this publication. If you don't know any young boys, then get to know some. Humor changes with each generation, as does what constitutes adventure. Short sentences—usually no more than one sentence per character each time a character speaks—is what this publication is looking for. Problems should be solved in these stories, but the solution must come from what happens within the story, not from a solution you impose upon the story. The story should definitely not read like a lecture from a parent.

10. *Adventure, mystery, action (a Christian truth must be interwoven into the story). Avoid moralistic and trite writing.* These stories should read like the Hardy Boys told from a Christian viewpoint. All religious information should be integrated so that it's a normal part of the boy's life. What the boy does in the story, how he behaves in different situations, should indicate his Christian viewpoint, rather than having somebody spout at him or read him quotes from the Bible.

11. *Action, fantasy, mystery, West Indian and African folklore, set in the past, present, or future. Informs and tries to instill the heritage of black culture, history, and pride into lives.* I don't subscribe to the opinion that you have to be black to write for black publications—I know too many white writers who've written for primarily black publications. But you most certainly have to be aware of what black publications are trying to do. This publication must be studied carefully.

12. Stories with universal settings, conflicts, and characters; children of other lands and cultures and religions; adventure stories; parables; moral building stories. Stories should focus on character-building qualities and should be wholesome without moralizing or preaching.   This publication will accept a very broad range of story types, as long as each story promotes indirectly a positive attitude toward traditional family life and ways to solve life's problems by living a wholesome life. This publication would also be a very good place for stories in which religions other than Christianity are the focus.

13. Stories in rhyme, easy-to-read stories for beginning readers, seasonals with holiday themes, realistic or fanciful plots, folktales, read-aloud stories. Avoid stereotyping. Characters should appear realistic. Stories about working mothers, single-parent homes, changing times.   This would be a very challenging publication to write for. On the one hand, it seems very attractive to a lot of beginning writers who want to write stories in verse, but who often turn out very dated stories, using information from their own childhood. The secret to success here is to make the subject matter as current as possible. A good story in good rhyme about a child's relationship with his working mother or his life in a single-parent home, for instance, would probably find immediate publication here.

14. Stories that appeal to both boys and girls, which the eight-to-twelve group will read, which will capture their interest in the first few sentences. Need stories for beginning readers which have strong plot and suspense, with short sentences and lots of action. Need stories with female leads, humorous, urban settings, adventure, other cultures and religions. No war, crime, or violence.   Pay very close attention to the taboos here, because almost any mystery or suspense/adventure story will have some crime or violence, so it'll take a lot of effort on your part not to include these in your story. This particular publication might accept a crime or mention of a crime *offstage*, but never anything in which the main characters are involved. Crime and violence must never seem to touch the main characters—a very tall order. This publication would also be a good place to send stories about religions other than Christianity.

15. *Experimental, mainstream, mystery, suspense/ adventure, science fiction, fantasy, humorous, religious, and historical fiction.* If you're interested in writing category short stories, this should be one of your first markets, since it's very open. *Experimental* is the key word here. It means that the editors will be willing to look at less traditional approaches to writing stories, even category stories.

16. *Realistic stories, fantasies, adventures set in the past, present, or future. Want good plots, strong structure, action, and humor.* Here, the type of story you write is less important to the editor than the fact that you have unique characters, settings, and plots. These stories should be strongly written. You must pay very close attention to the structural development of the story. (Chapter Fifteen, "Outlining Your Short Story," will be of special importance here.) This publication would also be a good place to send your historical short stories.

17. *Adventures that present characters working out their problems according to Biblical principles; adventures with religious, spiritual lessons or applications. No fictionalized Bible stories or events.* A good story for this publication would be a suspense/adventure set in a church camp where problems are worked out with direct references to passages in the Bible.

18. *Christian adventure . . . no mention of dancing, drinking, smoking, divorce, mixed swimming, use of television, sports of a professional nature, wearing of shorts or slacks for women.* Don't be put off by these editorial details. In fact, this would probably be an excellent market for a writer of religious fiction who's interested in writing about things he remembers from ten, twenty, or thirty years ago. These stories would be similar to those found in publications in the forties and fifties, or even earlier.

19. Nautical and oceanographic adventure, historical, humorous.   Don't think you have to live by an ocean to write for this publication. Books from your local library can help, but also remember that this publication will probably also accept stories involving boating on a lake in your area. Talk to some of the local boat owners and listen to their tales of adventure, then gear their tales to young readers.

20. Stories of heroism, adventure, nature; should stress principles of living right, such as good health habits, temperance, honesty, truthfulness, courtesy, purity, respect and love for parents and God.   Very seldom do you see the word *heroism* in editorial requirements, so I'd zero in on that if I were you. This publication would be interested in young people's rescuing other people from burning buildings or from tornado-ravaged homes. The editors would probably also be interested in a story about a young person who found a purse with a lot of money in it and returned it to the owner. The story should probably indicate that the young hero or heroine is putting to work the values instilled in him by his parents.

21. Christian character-building but not preachy; the hero or heroine should be eleven or twelve, in situations of one or more of the following: mystery; sports; adventure; school; travel; relationships with parents, friends, and others; animal stories (preferably dogs or horses).   A story in a wholesome setting would work here. A good bet would be a mystery or an adventure in which a horse or a dog played a prominent role. Any time you see animals listed in the editorial information, you can usually assume that the editors don't get many such stories.

22. Stories that provide patterns of forgiveness, respect, integrity, understanding, caring, sharing; God; Jesus; the Bible; prayer; death; heaven. A publication such as this would be interested in a story about the death of a young person and about how the other young people around this young person come to terms with it. Such a story could start with the diagnosis of an illness and carry the main character and his friends from that point to the death of the young friend. As such, it could almost be a blueprint of how young people can handle such situations.

23. Profiles of scientists and children; topical stories about animals, the environment, astronomy, and other areas of science. A lot of research would have to go into a story for this publication. But it must still be an entertaining story. A good story would be one about the life of a famous scientist as seen through the eyes of his children. How were their lives affected by their father's work? How were their lives different from those of other children? What was their attitude toward their father? Another type of story would be one in which a young person develops an interest in a particular area of science and decides to make this his career.

24. Picture stories, bedtime, naptime, easy-to-read stories, stories with educational value, health-related stories, and anthropomorphic animal stories. This would be a very good market for stories that teach as well as entertain. I've discovered that most editors of magazines for young people are always interested in coordinating the contents of their publications with school curricula.

Many editors of magazines for young people have on hand the curriculum guides for major school systems, such as those in Florida, Texas, California, and New York. They know at a glance what's being taught in those systems. The editor can consult the curriculum guides to see if the story he's interested in can be promoted as a supplement to a particular curriculum.

While it would be possible to write a curriculum-related story in all the categories I've discussed, it does seem to me that the mystery and suspense/adventure categories offer the best possibility for success.

Some of the school subjects around which mystery and suspense/adventure stories could be centered are:

a. English. English grammar holds some intriguing possibilities, especially for mystery stories. Why, for instance, do we use the forms *who, who-m,* and *who-se?* You could let grammatical *case* become your detective's *case!* Students would be much more likely to care about grammar if they could first read about it in a mystery story rather than in a grammar book.

b. Health studies. Phobias are a good source for mysteries in the area of health. Most phobias have long, complicated-looking names, but a mystery story giving the symptoms, then asking what causes the phobia, can simplify phobias creating an interest in solving phobia-related problems that young people often have.

c. History. History, too, can be the basis for interesting mystery and suspense/adventure stories for young people. Did Richard III really kill the Little Princes? The debate still rages. You can search history books for mysteries that remain unsolved or hidden treasures that haven't been found and turn the information into entertaining *and educational* short stories.

d. Science. This subject area offers one of the greatest possibilities for solutions to mysteries. There's especially a tremendous amount of material available in the area of forensic science, which is very much a part of crime-solving in most cities around the world. Almost every library will have at least one book on forensic (or police) science, that is, how police use science to solve crimes, but it might well pay you to invest in your own copy of a book on general forensic science so it'll always be handy.

Police contacts, while not necessarily a must, certainly offer you a depth of information. Now, I must admit that I have family connections to the Detroit Police Department, but even if you don't have similar connections, you can always find somebody who knows somebody who knows somebody who knows a policeman. Get them to introduce you. In my home town in Oklahoma, not only have I become acquainted (professionally!) with members of the local police department, I've also become acquainted with members of the F.B.I. and the Oklahoma State Bureau of Investigation. Things I've learned from these contacts have allowed me to give my stories authenticity. If you're a serious writer, almost any policeman will be glad to let you in on a few tricks of the trade.

Get to know teachers in the elementary schools in your area and find out from them what problems really bother their students in the area of science (or other school subjects, for that matter), then do research in those areas to try to find the plot for a story.

25. Short stories that motivate Jewish children toward learning about Judaism and help them find a place in the Jewish community as productive members. Editors are always interested in stories that celebrate Jewish holidays. You could have a non-Jewish friend visiting a Jewish friend during a holiday season and have the Jewish friend explain the significance of the holiday. Historical stories would find a home here, especially those that emphasize keeping alive Jewish beliefs.

Most published writers have been published because they've learned to master editorial requirements. If you master them—if you study the requirements, pay very close attention to them, and learn to read between the lines—then you, too, will be a published writer.

15

Outlining Your Short Story

An outline should be considered the very backbone of your short story. A good story-structure outline can save you a lot of agony during the actual writing of the story. It can keep you on track as you tell your tale, and it's a good hedge against writer's block.

But as a beginning writer you want to write. You want to get on with it! You don't want to be bothered with an outline. You're planning to sell a *story,* not an outline. What you need to realize, however, is that outlining *is* writing *and* a very important step in producing a good short story.

Most people, however, have had terrible experiences with outlines. Public school teachers have often been guilty of saying to their students, "Outline this book and turn it in to me tomorrow!" This was busywork, pure and simple, and accomplished nothing except to make students absolutely hate outlining. They'll write their papers first, then outline them, because an outline is required. Beginning writers are often guilty of taking the same approach with their short stories.

163

WRITING SHORT STORIES FOR YOUNG PEOPLE

Teachers usually require outlines of papers without really showing their students the importance of the outline. Students view the outline as a nuisance requirement, not as an aid to writing a better paper. I hope that after you've read this chapter, you, the beginning writer of short stories for young people, will see the need for outlining.

A good outline takes a lot of time and a lot of thought, but it's time and thought well spent. If a story is properly outlined, it'll be much easier to write. If you've outlined your story well, actually thought it through, then your outline will guide you through the writing of the story. This is not to say that modifications can't be made as you're writing. Just as we gain and lose weight, our backbones remain the same. So it is with the outline.

Let's look now at an outline that can be used (with modifications) for all the forms of stories that have been discussed.

OUTLINE FOR A SHORT STORY

I. Beginning (1-3 pages)

A. Setting described (working from the general to the specific)

B. Characters introduced
1. Major
a. Young People
b. Adults (not always needed)
c. Animals (not always needed)
2. Minor
a. Young People (not always needed)
b. Adults (not always needed)
c. Animals (not always needed)
3. Stock (usually appear once and may be introduced throughout the story)

C. Plot (problems to be solved) presented
1. Immediate problem
2. Ultimate problem (if one's desirable/called for)

II. Middle (5-10 pages)

A. First solution to the immediate problem
1. Complication 1
2. Complication 2
3. Complication 3 . . .

B. Second solution to the immediate problem (not always necessary)
1. Complication 1
2. Complication 2
3. Complication 3 . . .

C. Climax (final complication)
1. Realization of what must be done to solve immediate problem and ultimate problem (if it's being considered)
2. Character change brought about by realization (if an ultimate problem is to be included in the plot)
3. Actual attempt to solve immediate problem and ultimate problem (if there's one)
   a. Subcomplication 1
   b. Subcomplication 2
   c. Subcomplication 3

III. End (1-3 pages)

A. Immediate problem solved

B. Major character searches for way to prove he's changed (if an ultimate problem is to be included in the plot)

C. Solution to ultimate problem (if there's one)

To illuminate this outline, I'll analyze one of my stories that appeared in *Jack and Jill,* "Escape from East Berlin."

Escape from East Berlin

BY GEORGE EDWARD STANLEY

"We'll never get out of East Berlin without our passports," Alexandra Waterford said. "That has to be the dumbest thing you've ever done!"

"I only put your purse down for a minute while I was in the powder room before we left the opera," Cathy Waterford said. "How was I to know that somebody would steal our passports from it?"

It was at times such as these that Catherine Waterford wished that her parents were still alive and that she hadn't come to Europe to live with her older sister, Alexandra. Alexandra simply didn't understand how things like this could happen to thirteen-year-olds.

They were standing at the corner of *Friedrichstrasse* and *Französische Strasse* in East Berlin. The streets were dark and deserted. The West Berlin border was only six blocks away, but it might as well have been sixty.

Then suddenly, they could hear a rumbling noise below them.

"What's that?" Cathy asked.

"It's the *U-Bahn*," Alexandra said, pointing to the *U-Bahn* sign in the middle of the intersection. "There's the entrance to the station."

Cathy brightened.

"That gives me an idea," she said. "I know how we can get out of East Berlin!"

"The *U-Bahn* is the *West* Berlin subway, Catherine," Alexandra said. "The trains come through East Berlin, but they don't stop anymore. Besides, there are always armed guards to keep people from trying to get on the trains."

"I know, Alexandra," Cathy said. "I've ridden them before, remember? Anyway, we're not going to take the train; we're going to use the tunnel."

"Are you crazy?" Alexandra said. "We'll be shot!"

But Cathy had already crossed the intersection and was going down the steps to the entrance. Alexandra followed reluctantly. Cathy opened the door to the entrance slightly. The station was dimly lit.

"There's a guard standing at the edge of the platform," she whispered. "He's holding a machine gun. The train's going north toward *Friedrichstrasse* Station. We can go through the opposite tunnel."

"I don't believe I'm doing this," Alexandra moaned.

While the guard's attention was on the slow-moving train, Cathy pulled Alexandra unnoticed into the semi-darkness of the station platform.

The train had begun to pick up speed. The guard followed it with his eyes and his machine gun. As the last car entered the tunnel, the guard turned and started walking back to the inspector's office in the middle of the platform.

Cathy grabbed Alexandra's hand, and they rushed to the edge of the platform, the noise of their footsteps covered by the sound of the departing train. Cathy sat down on the edge of the platform and swung her legs over the edge to the bottom. She almost fell when she hit the ground. Alexandra followed. They stumbled into the darkness of the tunnel.

As they felt their way along the walls of the tunnel, the dim light of the *Französische Strasse* Station began to disappear. They could hear only the sound of their breathing and the whispers of the air as it rushed back into the tunnel, after having been displaced by the train.

"The next station will be in West Berlin," Cathy said, "and it'll be brightly lit. We're no more than six blocks from the West Berlin border."

Then from behind them the air began to move again, first as a whisper, then as a wind, growing stronger. In the distance they could hear a slight rumbling sound.

"Oh dear," Cathy said. "I thought we could get through the tunnel before another train came along."

"Now what are we going to do?" Alexandra asked.

"The tracks evidently run parallel," Cathy said. "They only

seem to separate when they get to the stations. All we have to do is stay against the wall on the side opposite the train, and we'll be fine."

"Oh, sure," Alexandra said, but she followed Cathy and flattened herself against the opposite wall.

The rumbling was getting louder. The force of the air being pushed toward them was stronger. The earth had begun to vibrate, and the light of the train's engine was beginning to illuminate their part of the tunnel. The rumbling had become so great that Cathy was sure they'd be shaken onto the tracks of the oncoming train. They covered their ears, and then the train was upon them. Alexandra screamed. The lights of the cars flashed images on the walls about them like a projector gone mad. And then it was over. The rumbling died down. The air changed directions.

They began to feel their way through the tunnel again, watching the red taillight of the train disappear. Suddenly the red light turned to white.

"That white light must be the station," Cathy said. "That must be West Berlin!"

Alexandra started walking faster. Cathy followed. The light began to get larger as they approached. But not brighter. Cathy was puzzled. Alexandra was almost pulling her through the tunnel. They would soon get to the station. The tracks had separated. They were following the southbound tracks into West Berlin. The tunnel had narrowed. Then another rumbling sound began. It would be a train coming from the other direction on the northbound tracks, headed for East Berlin. It would stop at the station for passengers on the other side of the platform.

The rumbling of the train continued as they made their way toward the light of the station. What was wrong? Cathy wondered. The station wasn't lit brightly enough, and the train didn't seem to be stopping. They had reached the opening of the tunnel. On the other side of the station platform, they could see the slow-moving train. Standing alone on the platform in the dimly lit station was a guard holding a machine gun. He was watching the train pass. They were still in East Berlin!

They retreated into the tunnel just as the last car of the train left the station.

"What's wrong?" Alexandra asked. "I thought you said this station would be in *West* Berlin!"

"It must be right on the border," Cathy said. "We're probably not more than a few feet from West Berlin. We'll just have to wait until another train comes along on the other side so that the guard will have his back to us."

"What about the trains passing on *this* side?" Alexandra asked. "The tunnel's too narrow here for them to pass without hitting us."

"Oh dear," Cathy said, "I forgot about that!"

So they walked back into the tunnel to where the tracks paralleled and waited until a southbound train had passed; then they returned to the station entrance. Alexandra had begun to shiver. At last, they heard the northbound train approaching.

"As soon as it enters the station," Cathy said, "we need to run toward the opposite tunnel. Keep low along the platform so you won't be seen in case the guard decides to turn around."

"Don't worry, Catherine," Alexandra said huffily, "I'm getting rather good at this."

As the train entered the station, Cathy began running toward the opposite tunnel. Alexandra followed. Midway along the platform, Alexandra fell over a cable and cried out in pain. Cathy turned. The guard had also turned away from the train and was staring straight at them, not believing what he was seeing. Alexandra was up in an instant and was limping toward the entrance to the tunnel. Cathy held out her hand for her.

"Halten Sie! Halten Sie!" the guard shouted.

He started firing his machine gun. The bullets bounced off the walls of the tunnel. But Cathy and Alexandra continued to run. Cathy was almost pulling Alexandra through the tunnel. Their lives now depended on how far ahead of the guard they could keep. Behind them, they could hear the sound of his heavy boots on the ground. In front of them, they could see a very bright light. West Berlin! And then they felt it. A sudden rush of air and the familiar rumble. A train was coming from behind them. If they stopped to let the train pass, the guard would catch them. If they continued running, they would reach the narrow part of the tunnel where the tracks separated. There would be no place for them to stand so that the train could pass without hitting them.

Up ahead, the lights of the station were getting larger; behind them, the rumbling of the train was getting louder. Cathy was almost dragging Alexandra through the tunnel. She looked back and could see the yellow light of the train's engine. It was just a speck in the darkness, but she knew it would grow rapidly. Would the guard follow them, she wondered, or would he stop and let the train pass?

"Faster, Alexandra, faster!" Cathy shouted.

They couldn't stop now. They ran toward the station. They were nearing the entrance. Just a few more feet. Behind them, the train rushed through the darkness.

Then suddenly there were shouts and screams as the people standing on the platform saw them. Cathy pulled Alexandra to the edge of the platform to outstretched hands just as the train hurtled past them.

They were pulled exhausted onto the platform by astonished West Berliners waiting for their trains. The station inspector took them to his office, where he gave them some blankets and hot coffee.

"Now then," he said, as they began drinking their second cups of coffee, "why don't you tell me all about it?"

In the first two pages of your story, you must do three things: 1) describe the setting; 2) introduce the characters; and 3) present the plot. Let's look at the first part of "Escape from East Berlin" and see how this was accomplished.

I've always felt that it's very important to let a reader know immediately where he is—a haunted house, a forest, or a foreign city. Certain images start forming in the reader's mind as soon as he is oriented geographically, and the writer benefits from this. East Berlin is mentioned not only in the title of the story but also in the first sentence. Besides actually labeling the city in which the story takes place, East Berlin is being used as a mnemonic device. The reader probably knows about East Berlin—especially The Wall—from school, from movies, and from television. Upon reading it, certain images should be created in his mind. It's very helpful to a writer for his reader to be able to create these images. Mnemonic devices, then, are important, because they allow you to keep your geographical descriptions to a minimum (after all, you're not writing a travel guide) and at the same time create the atmosphere via the geographical setting you want to create. Sometimes, as with East Berlin, the name of the city alone is enough to create this atmosphere. In a short story, where you're limited to a certain number of words, this is very important. Other cities can often do the same thing for writers: New York, Paris, Rome—all are good examples because they are all places that young readers are familiar with from other sources. If you'll take advantage of mnemonic devices, then you can let the reader help you create part of the setting.

In the fourth paragraph of the story, I go from the general setting to the specific setting. I go from naming East Berlin to pinpointing the corner of *Friedrichstrasse* and *Französische Strasse*. This is an establishing shot, and in this sense, I'm doing the same thing a motion picture does when it begins with an aerial view of Manhattan (or some other city), then zooms in on a particular skyscraper or street corner. I used the actual German names for the streets because I feel that any story set in a foreign country should use some foreign words for flavor. You should be cautioned, however, that this can be overdone. The meaning of the words should be obvious even though they're in a foreign language. Here, these words are obviously the names of streets.

Finally, I used some descriptive adjectives to assure the mood I wanted to create—*dark and deserted;* added a comment about West Berlin's border's being only six blocks away to create a feeling of "so near, yet so far"; and the setting has been established. This has all been done with a minimum of words, but the reader is now firmly oriented geographically.

Within these first two pages, the characters must also be introduced. Go easy on the number of characters. You don't want to have too many for yourself or your readers to have to contend with. I generally like to have two major characters who can work off each other—two characters who for some reason don't usually see eye to eye. If you populate your story with too many characters, it'll be very easy to lose control of them. You'll have them doing too much or too little.

There are three types of characters; *major, minor,* and *stock.* The most important characters are the major characters; the story is written around them. Minor characters interact with major characters, although they're not on stage as much as the major characters. Major and minor characters should be introduced in the beginning of the story. Stock characters are characters who usually appear one time in a story. They may be introduced anywhere during the story. Stock characters are important and should be considered carefully, as they add verisimilitude to your story; however, you don't have to worry about fleshing them out or giving them motivations as you do with the major and minor characters.

In "Escape from East Berlin," the first character introduced is Alexandra Waterford. She's a major character and is introduced in the first sentence. In a short story, this is a very good idea. You need to get your people on stage as quickly as possible— better yet, they should already be on stage when you start writing. You shouldn't have to worry about setting up an entrance for them. It's also important that the reader know something about the characters as soon as possible. The name Alexandra itself suggests somebody formal. Again, I'm using a word (as with *East*

Berlin) to suggest something to my reader. This allows me to use fewer descriptive words in favor of more action words later. Alexandra states "That has to be the dumbest thing you've ever done!" The reader infers that she has little or no tolerance for other people's mistakes.

In the next paragraph, Cathy Waterford is introduced. She's the second major character, and her name suggests something about her as well. Instead of using Catherine, I use Cathy, and immediately the reader feels that this character is less formal than her sister. Cathy's statement about "losing the passports" makes us feel that she's probably very vulnerable and that things like this probably plague her life.

The third paragraph is the only direct characterization paragraph in the story. It's here that I make clear why Cathy is in Europe in the first place and that Alexandra doesn't understand thirteen-year-olds. With the exception of this one paragraph, all the other information about the characters has been integrated into the story, that is, it's been given *indirectly* to the reader. Again, this is very important. You may have to stop and narrate some information about the characters, but it shouldn't be more than a paragraph. The rest of the information about them should be given indirectly, through names or through conversations that the characters themselves have.

"Escape from East Berlin" has no minor characters. An example of a minor character I could have used in the story would be that of a secret policeman. If I'd started the story at the opera with the discovery of the missing passports, I could have had a secret policeman shadowing Cathy and Alexandra as they searched East Berlin (without seeming to do so) for a means of escape to West Berlin. They could have given him the slip just long enough to get into the *U-Bahn* station at *Friedrichstrasse* and *Französische Strasse* before he suspected where they'd gone (perhaps he saw the door closing) and then he could have followed them into the tunnel, not necessarily sounding a general alarm (he would have known about the next *U-Bahn* station that was still in East Berlin). . . . But as you can see, I'm changing the story a lot—and that's what a minor character can do. Even though the story isn't written

173

around a minor character, minor characters do interact with major characters and can have a decided effect on how the story actually turns out.

There are, however, three stock characters in my story: 1) the first *U-Bahn* station guard, a *Vopo,* that is, *Volkspolizei,* meaning people's police; 2) the second *Vopo;* and 3) the West Berlin *U-Bahn* station inspector. These characters appear at only one place in the story.

The plot is the third element that must be introduced in the first two pages of a short story. The plot is the problem (or problems) that must be solved. There are two types of problems, immediate and ultimate. Of course, in a story that's meant mainly to entertain, the plot is generally what interests the reader first. Seldom is the reader of popular fiction primarily interested in character development or in setting. In a short story, the immediate problem should be presented in the first paragraph. In "Escape from East Berlin," it comes in the first sentence: *"We'll never get out of East Berlin without our passports," Alexandra Waterford said.* The immediate problem to be solved, then, is: *How are Alexandra and Cathy going to get out of East Berlin without their passports?* You have in that question the setting, the characters, and the immediate problem. In fact, you should be able to incorporate all three elements into a question such as this before you write the beginning of your story. Outlining the story first will help you accomplish this.

For most stories written strictly for entertainment, it's necessary to consider only the immediate problem of the plot. Readers of entertainment fiction are generally not interested in any ultimate problems in the story, that is, how an experience will change the major characters' lives. For instance, Cathy may or may not be more careful next time with the passports. And Alexandra will probably continue to be as stuffy and as hard to get along with as she always has been. These things don't really matter to the readers of the story. What matters is: *How are Alexandra and Cathy going to get out of East Berlin without their passports?,* the immediate problem.

Often, however, you'll want to include an ultimate problem as part of your plot—how the experiences of the immediate

174

problem will affect the lives of the major characters. Of all the categories of stories I've discussed, the mainstream story usually deals with this aspect the most. Of course, any type of story that I've discussed can incorporate such information, and in doing so, add dimensions to the story and the characters and put the story into some readers' (and some editors') classification as being more literary. For purposes of clarity, though, I'll stick to two types of stories: those written for sheer entertainment, in which the immediate problem is paramount; and those written for the emotional experience, for the sharing of ideas, for the development of characters, in which the ultimate problem is also considered. The writer chooses the type of story he wants to write. There's a market for both.

Let's look at a situation in which the writer (and perhaps the reader) is interested in how an immediate problem will affect a character—a situation in which both immediate and ultimate problems will be considered. You're writing a story about a young boy who's completely dominated by his father. Perhaps the father and son are on a fishing trip and are staying in an isolated mountain cabin. Maybe the father is a tyrant, maybe he isn't, but the father's word is law. He's the one who makes all the decisions. He's never wrong; no one challenges him in any matter. Then, one evening, the cabin is invaded by escaped convicts, and the father and son are held hostage. Such a scenario would set up a situation in which both immediate and ultimate problems could be considered. The immediate problem, of course, is how to get rid of the escaped convicts and get the lives of the major characters back to normal—as normal as possible. The ultimate problem would concern the reaction of the father to the situation. If, as I've indicated, he's always been the undisputed head of the family, it would be normal for the son to look to the father for a solution to the immediate problem. But let's say the father collapses under pressure from the situation. Let's say he's terrified by what's happened. He suddenly shows himself to be weak and afraid and indecisive when confronted with the terrifying situation of having the mountain cabin taken over by escaped convicts. What, then, will happen to his image now? How will he be viewed by the son, especially if it's the son who finally resolves the immediate problem—getting rid of the convicts? What will their relationship be like now? Things can't simply drift back to normal. The son will no longer consider the father as the strong leader of the family, the one person who has all the answers. The father has been stripped of his authority. He's been shown to be weak and indecisive. He's no longer the all-powerful figure that he once was. He knows it and the son knows it. How will the son react toward him now? Will the son respect his father? Well, maybe not at first. It will depend on how the father himself acts. The father must make the first move. Will the father try to regain control, or will he admit that he doesn't always have the right answers—and never did? These are some of the things that you would have to decide, if you're considering both immediate and ultimate problems in a story.

To help decide if ultimate problems should be considered, you should try to read as many stories in as many issues as possible of the publication you're writing for. If the publication uses mostly immediate-problem stories, you shouldn't include ultimate problems in your stories. If the publication likes for the major characters to solve both immediate and ultimate problems, then they should both be considered. Publications for young people will generally tell you in the writer's guidelines that, in addition to the main character's solving the immediate problem, he should also solve an ultimate problem, the latter being something that will teach him a lesson and make him a better person.

The middle part of the story should contain the solution to the plot—that is, how the main characters plan to solve the immediate problem—with its complications and its climax. The climax is actually the last complication in the solution to the problem, though it's the most complex of the complications because it has subcomplications.

When the main characters are presented with a problem, they must figure out how to solve it. One of the characters usually suggests a solution to the problem. This suggestion is then followed by three or four (approximately) unsuccessful attempts to solve the problem, followed by a last successful attempt—the climax. The climax is the point at which the main characters realize what must finally be done in order to solve the plot—the immediate problem. If an ultimate problem is being considered, then it's at this point that a character change is brought about by this realization. This is followed in turn by the actual attempt to solve the problem. This last complication on the way to solving the plot—the climax—is fraught with subcomplications before the problem is finally resolved.

In longer stories, instead of having one solution to an immediate problem, there can be two or even three, each having its own complications. The climax would still be the last complication of the last solution to the problem.

In "Escape from East Berlin," it's Cathy who suggests the first (and only) solution to the problem. When she hears the rumbling underneath her, she suggests to Alexandra that they can escape by using the *U-Bahn,* the underground train system operated by the West Berlin authorities. (If you're surprised to learn that the *U-Bahn* is still allowed to operate underground in East Berlin, then you might also be surprised to learn that the *S-Bahn,* the aboveground train system owned and operated by East Berlin, also operates in West Berlin. West Berliners, however, for the most part, avoid riding the *S-Bahn.* East Berliners *can't* ride the *U-Bahn.*)

The solution to the problem is misunderstood by Alexandra, who knows that, although the *U-Bahn* still runs through East Berlin, the stations are closed to keep people out. Cathy realizes this, too, but what she has in mind isn't the normal activity of riding a subway train. She's planning to use the tunnels through which to make their escape! Alexandra thinks this is a crazy idea, but because she's desperate, she goes along with it.

Now that I have the first suggested solution to the problem, I need to introduce the complications to the solution. In order to use the tunnels for escape, Cathy and Alexandra must first get down into them. The first complication to the solution, then, concerns how they're going to get into the *U-Bahn* station. These stations are little islands in the middle of the streets. They're surrounded by wrought-iron fences with gates.

If you'll remember in Chapter Thirteen, "Collecting Information and Ideas," I made reference to how very important it is for writers to keep their eyes and ears open. I conceived the idea for

"Escape from East Berlin" while riding the *U-Bahn* under East Berlin itself. I noticed the guards in the dimly-lit stations, with their machine guns pointed toward the trains. I noticed men in the tunnels, working on the tracks, so I knew that people could actually walk through the tunnels. I also knew that I'd never heard of anybody trying to use the tunnels for escape. All of these observations came together in the story "Escape from East Berlin." But from these observations on, I had to rely on fiction. I don't really know if the doors to the stations are kept unlocked or not. Frankly, I had no intention of walking over to one of the stations to find out. For that, I could still be in an East German jail. (There is a limit to what I'll do to gain authenticity for my stories!) But I don't think that I'm stretching imagination too far if I choose to have the gate to the fence open (they're low enough that they could be vaulted if necessary, anyway) and the door to the station unlocked. (Most East Berliners would probably know what could be waiting for them if they attempted to escape this way, but the innocence and naiveté of foreigners can often be used to great advantage in fiction!) And it wouldn't be too unusual for the guards to be so preoccupied or bored or lazy that they had become complacent. And since the story takes place at night, it wouldn't be impossible for two people to slip unseen from the sidewalk to the center of a deserted street, go down the steps of the station, and hide just long enough to be able to open the door slowly to see what lies beyond them—*and bring us to our second complication.*

The second complication consists of getting from the station entrance across the platform to the tunnel itself. In getting past this complication, Cathy and Alexandra are helped by a passing train. They open the door to the station, see the guard watching the train, slip into the station, and rush to the edge of the platform. They sit down, swing their legs off, and run into the tunnel. *Whew!,* you hope your reader is saying. The guard didn't see them. They got from the street to the entrance and from the entrance to the tunnel. Now all they have to do is run through the tunnel and they'll be safe, won't they? Well, *we now come to the third complication.*

Cathy and Alexandra are now in the tunnel. Seemingly,

we've reached the last complication—getting through the tunnel to the next *U-Bahn* station in West Berlin. This is, however, at this point, an incomplete (false) complication. As they begin their slow journey through the darkened tunnel, Cathy and Alexandra feel a sudden rush of air from behind them. Behind them, too, they can hear a slight rumbling noise. A train is coming! If you've ever been in a subway station before a train arrives, you'll recall that there *is* a sudden rush of air as the train displaces it through the tunnel. This is accompanied by a rumbling of the earth. The third complication, then, is to get through the tunnel without getting hit by the subway train. Since the tracks run parallel and separate only when they get to a station, Cathy suggests that they stand against the opposite wall to avoid the oncoming train. They aren't prepared, however, for the terrifying experience of being in a tunnel as a train rushes by. (The trains go slowly only through the East Berlin stations; otherwise, they travel very fast indeed!) Finally, the train has passed and another complication has been resolved. Cathy and Alexandra resume their journey toward East Berlin.

Again, the reader may think that Cathy and Alexandra have made it, that it's only a matter of coming from the darkness of the tunnel to the lights of West Berlin. But again, there's a surprise for the reader; *the fourth complication.*

Cathy and Alexandra see a dim light ahead of them and think that it must be the next station, in West Berlin. They begin walking faster. But something is wrong. If the station is in West Berlin, the light really should be getting brighter. But the light doesn't get brighter, even as Cathy and Alexandra near the entrance to the station. They also hear a rumbling sound. Another train is coming. But this time, it'll stop at the station, they think. The fourth complication, then, is simply (!) to make it to the next *U-Bahn* station (which they still think is in West Berlin) while the train is stopped.

They reach the end of the island station. But the light isn't brighter and the train doesn't seem to be stopping. The tracks have separated and will now go on both sides of the platform. This is the narrow part of the tunnel. Cathy and Alexandra run breathlessly through the tunnel *by the platform opposite the train* into the

U-Bahn station. Are they now past the fourth complication? Yes! Are they now safely in West Berlin? No!

Cathy and Alexandra suddenly realize *why* the lights of the station hadn't gotten any brighter and *why* the train hadn't stopped. They're still in East Berlin! (I need to point out here that this complication also arises from observation. On this particular subway line, on *Friedrichstrasse,* which leads, by the way, to Checkpoint Charlie, there is a *U-Bahn* station just a few feet from the border crossing.)

Cathy and Alexandra are now presented with *a fifth complication:* they must either stay in the station or go back into the tunnel. They can't stay in the station. When the train has finally passed, they'll be seen by the *Vopo.* And they can't simply retreat a short distance into the tunnel: it's too narrow and they'll be killed by the trains coming from the opposite direction. They rush back to where the tracks separate to allow the trains to pass and themselves to think.

Complication five has now been solved in short order. Since there has already been a harrowing train experience, this one can be handled in a few sentences. It's important that the trains continue to run at what would be normal intervals, though, in order to maintain verisimilitude in the story.

We have now reached the climax of the story. I won't be using Part B from the outline in this story, as Cathy and Alexandra haven't give up their first solution to the immediate problem: they're still trying to escape by using the tunnel. To use Part B, I would have had Cathy and Alexandra give up their first solution, go back to where they started, the first *U-Bahn* station, exit it, and come up with a new way of getting out of East Berlin. In longer stories (and especially in novels), this is done. If I were to do this in "Escape from East Berlin," I could have Cathy or Alexandra suggest a land route, swimming cross the River Spree, taking a plane, or even using a hot air balloon as a means of escape!

The climax is the final attempt to solve the plot and the final complication to the problem. It's at this point that the main characters realize what must be done to solve the immediate problem (and if you're considering it, the ultimate problem, too). The climax is a complex complication, which has its own subcomplications.

Once they've had time to think about it, Cathy and Alexandra realize that the next step (the final step to freedom) will be to walk through the *U-Bahn* station in full view of the *Vopo*. They also know that they must wait until a train is passing and has the guard's attention. They'll then go through the tunnel on the opposite side. In other words, the guard will have his back to the side of the platform by which Cathy and Alexandra will be passing. This is the climax, *the final complication*—to walk through the *U-Bahn* station while the guard is watching a train pass on the opposite side of the platform.

Cathy and Alexandra walk to the edge of the station entrance. They wait. They hear the train. When it starts passing slowly through the station, they crouch low, walking on the tracks at the edge of the platform, and start through the station. Now I introduce the first *subcomplication:* Alexandra trips over a cable, falls, and cries out in pain. The guard turns toward her. Cathy helps Alexandra up and they start running. The guard starts chasing them, firing his machine gun into the darkness of the tunnel. Can they outrun him? Can they solve this subcomplication to their getting from the last *U-Bahn* station in East Berlin to the next *U-Bahn* station in West Berlin? Now here, I could simply have a chase scene and see who could outrun whom. But I can't forget that the trains are running regularly, so I introduce *a second subcomplication:* another train, also coming from behind them. If they continue running toward West Berlin, they'll reach the narrow part of the tunnel, where the tracks are separated, and may be crushed by the train. If they stop and let the train pass, the *Vopo* will catch them. They have to make a split-second decision. They continue running! Maybe, just maybe, they'll reach the station in West Berlin before the train does. This running scene is handled in four short paragraphs to convey the rapidity with which it's taking place. At the end of the fourth paragraph, Cathy and Alexandra reach the edge of the station platform just as the train hurtles by them.

The end of the story is generally handled in one or two pages; it allows the writer and the reader to tie up any loose ends—

if there are any. This is also the point in the story where you can show how the main character has changed, thus proving that the ultimate problem has been solved. As I mentioned earlier, if the story is written mainly for entertainment, the reader will have little interest in whether or not the major characters have had learning experiences. In "Escape from East Berlin," any learning experiences are of little or no importance. What these last pages let the reader know is that Cathy and Alexandra are indeed safely back in West Berlin, and that's all the reader wanted to know in the first place. He finds out that Cathy and Alexandra are pulled from the tracks just in time, then taken by the station inspector to his office, where he wraps them in blankets and gives them something hot to drink. This ending, actually, is not an uncommon one; endings of this type are often seen on television and in the movies. After the main character has had a very harrowing experience and is finally safe, someone says, "Now, then, why don't you just relax and start at the beginning?" This is another established device, like a motion picture fadeout, that lets the reader know that the story is over. He doesn't expect anything else.

Now let's look at the original outline, adding the story elements to the outline elements:

OUTLINE FOR "ESCAPE FROM EAST BERLIN"

I. Beginning: Paragraphs 1-4

    A. Setting: East Berlin, corner of *Friedrichstrasse* and *Französische Strasse,* dark and deserted, West Berlin border six blocks away

    B. Characters
        1 Major
            a. Young people: Cathy Waterford, Alexandra Waterford
            b. Adults: None
            c. Animals: None
        2. Minor: None

    3. Stock: 1st *Vopo*, 2nd *Vopo*, West Berlin Station Inspector

C. Plot

    1. Immediate problem: To get out of East Berlin without passports

    2. Ultimate problem: None

II. Middle: Paragraphs 5-45

A. First solution: To use *U-Bahn* tunnel for escape

    1. Complication 1: To get from street to *U-Bahn* station entrance

    2. Complication 2: To get from station entrance, past 1st *Vopo*, across platform, to tunnel

    3. Complication 3: To get through tunnel without being hit by subway train

    4. Complication 4: To get through tunnel to the next *U-Bahn* station while train is stopped

    5. Complication 5: To stay in East Berlin *U-Bahn* station and be captured or to go back into tunnel and risk being hit by subway train.

B. Second solution: None

C. Climax

    1. Realization of what must be done to solve immediate problem: To walk through East Berlin *U-Bahn* station while 2nd *Vopo* is watching train.

    2. Character change: None

    3. Actual attempt to solve immediate problem:

        a. Subcomplication 1: Alexandra trips and falls, and 2nd *Vopo* starts chasing them with machine gun

        b. Subcomplication 2· Another train is coming from behind them

III. End: Paragraphs 46-48

A. Solution to immediate problem: Cathy and Alexandra reach

West Berlin platform in time and are pulled to safety as train hurtles by
B. Major character searches for way to prove he's changed: None
C. Solution to ultimate problem: None

You can see that the structure of the outline has been maintained throughout the story. The major modifications have concerned the ultimate problem. I chose in "Escape from East Berlin" not to consider any ultimate problems.

For those writers who think that an outline will inhibit their free spirit, their literary flow, let me say this: both editors and readers expect stories, especially those classified as category fiction, to contain the required elements of the categories I have discussed in chapters Three through Ten. These elements must always be in your story or you won't be able to call it a mystery or a fantasy or a romance, or whatever it is that you think you're writing. It's really not up to you, especially if you're not an established writer, to change these structures. Even established writers who experiment with different structures for the various categories run the risk of alienating their readers. Readers are very demanding people (and as a writer, you certainly can't do without readers!). It *is* your task, however, to weave new and exciting tales around an already established structure. They are what will sell. And using a story structure outline is one of the major steps.

16

Characters and Characterization

Let's look now at the characters you're going to use in your stories. The first thing you should keep in mind is that you don't want too many of them. In fact, you usually don't need as many as you think you do. I've often written stories with more characters than I actually needed, only to have to go back and kill some of them off and give their dialogue to the remaining characters. That's one way of depopulating a story.

If you're beginning your story and think you have too many characters but don't know which ones to get rid of, then forget about it and go ahead and write your story with all of them. After you've finished the story, you can go back and see if you can possibly give any of the dialogue to other characters.

I once had a terrible time starting a story until I realized that I had one character too many. I gave this character's job to some-

185

one else, and the story took off. It's absolutely amazing what you can do with fewer characters. Beginning writers often think they're better off with a lot of characters in a story, but what they forget is that they have to develop all these characters. Every character must have things to do and something to say. You're much better off if you spend your writing time developing fewer characters.

You'll need to know your characters very well. You can do this by keeping a profile of them, in the form of a *Character Bio Sheet*. If you have a Character Bio Sheet filled out for each of the characters in your story, then you will not only be able to prevent your characters from doing things out of character, you'll also find that writing your story will be a lot easier.

I'm including here a sample of a possible Character Bio Sheet, which will help you get to know your characters better. You don't have to use this particular form, however; you can simply make up your own, if you want to.

CHARACTER BIO SHEET

1. Name of short story _____

2. Name of character _____

3. Age _____ Birth date _____ Birthplace _____

4. General appearance (*height, weight; color of eyes, hair, complexion*) _____
_____

5. Gestures _____

6. Sound of voice (*shrill, husky, etc.*) _____

7. Highest grade achieved in school _____

8. Subject which causes the most satisfaction _____

9. Subject which causes the most difficulty _____

10. Favorite words or expressions _____

11. Favorite clothes (*including make-up, jewelry, cologne, etc.*) _____

12. Favorite/least favorite colors _____

13. Favorite relatives. Why? _____

14. Favorite friends. Why? _____

15. Favorite pets _____

16. Favorite television shows/movies _____

17. Favorite/least favorite foods _____

18. Favorite books _____

19. Favorite music _____

20. Favorite types of cars _____

21. Things that make him/her laugh _____

22. Jealousies _____

23. What does room look like (*condition of closet, posters on the walls, etc.*)? _____
_____

24. Talents (*including sports*) _____

25. What does character fantasize about? _____

26. Most admirable personality traits (*independent, secure, etc.*). _____
_____

27. Least admirable personality traits (*dependent, insecure, etc.*). _____

28. Previous relations with the opposite sex (*and this doesn't necessarily mean* sexual *relations!*) _____
_____

29. How does character behave in a crisis? _____
_____

30. What makes this character angry? _____

31. How does this character show his anger? _____
_____

32. How does this character perceive himself/herself?
_____

33. How do other family members perceive this character? _____
_____

34. How do friends perceive this character? _____
_____

35. How do teachers perceive this character? _____
_____

36. How would character like to change his/her life?
_____

CHARACTERS AND CHARACTERIZATION

37. What are character's plans for the future? _____
   _____

38. What is character's greatest satisfaction? _____
   _____

39. What is character's problem at beginning of story?
   _____

These Character Bio Sheets should also be written for your minor characters, even though you may not need all the information in your story.

To the young people reading your story, there's actually nothing more important than your characters. These are the people they identify with; they're the center of the story. And each story you write will develop from the solution the main character comes up with.

That's why understanding point-of-view is so important. Most short stories for young people are written from a single point-of-view, because using that technique is the best way to achieve immediate reader identification. The only shifts in your point-of-view should be for brief passages of narration to move the story along. If you write a story from a multiple point-of-view, even if you have room for it, chances are you're tampering with making your young reader schizophrenic! Young people like to identify with the main character—with the main character's successes and failures—and multiple points-of-view only confuse the issue and at the same time force you to develop them in a limited space.

You'll be writing your story either in first person (using the pronoun *I*) or in third person (using the pronouns *he, she,* and *they*), and the viewpoint you choose will often be determined by the story itself. I've often debated as to whether first person or third person would work better in a particular story I was writing. One of the best ways to decide this is to take a page of whatever you've written and write it again using the other person. For me, one's always easier. The story seems to go faster. I'm not quite sure what it is within us or within the story that determines this, but the story itself will come out much more easily in one of the persons. You'll find yourself thinking faster and typing faster. The characters will be saying the things you want them to say better and more easily in one person than in the other. In short, which person you use can be determined for you if you'll just give each a chance.

The viewpoint should be introduced immediately. You can do this by starting the first sentence of your story with the pronoun *I*, if you're using first person. If you're using third person, you can start the first sentence of your story with the name of the main character, Mary Russell, for instance, followed in the next sentence by the pronoun *she*. The reader knows immediately who the story is about and can start trying to fit comfortably into the main character's point-of-view.

The first person viewpoint is more personal and intimate, and it gives the reader the feeling that he really knows the narrator of the story, who is usually the main character and the character that you want your reader to know well. So, editors of publications for young people usually like stories written in the first person. The first person point-of-view can be limiting, though. You're able to see the world only through the narrator's eyes, and if you want to inject any of your philosophy into the story, you have to do it through the mouths of your characters as they reveal *their* philosophies. In first person, because you have to stay inside the head of the main character, your reader will often not know what's going on in the story before the narrator does. (There are, of course, times when a limited narrator can describe what he himself doesn't understand, thereby making the information available to the reader, who will understand. In *Ben and Me,* Robert Lawson used this technique with Amos, a mouse who narrates the story.)

You may have read that there's a bias against using first person in stories. At one time, this was true—and to a certain extent it's still true in adult stories—but it's now quite commonplace to use first person in stories for young people because of the instant identification it allows. Adult readers don't need this immediate character identification, but young readers do, and using first person is one of the fastest ways to get the reader into the minds of the main characters, so that the reader can feel what the main characters are feeling.

Of course, you may certainly use third person, but doing so further distances the characters from the reader. If you're using third person, then you, as the writer, can see more of what's going on in the story, which means that your reader as well will see more of what's going on. You're able to move back and forth from character to character and give broader insights to the story.

There's actually a third choice you have when selecting the point-of-view for your story. This is the limited-third-person point-of-view, that is, using third person but maintaining a single viewpoint. The third person won't refer only to the main character. You won't be inside the head of the main character, as with first person, *but the reader will see everything from the main character's point-of-view.* Even though you're still staying very close to the main character, this point-of-view is much less restrictive to you, the writer.

A lot of beginning writers have trouble with their characters because they pattern them after real people. Let's face it—if the characters in stories weren't larger than life, we probably wouldn't read the stories. Characters should be composites of people you know or have read about, and they should jump out of the pages of your story, larger than life. You can often create such characters by taking the most outstanding physical features, personality traits, mental capabilities, and the like of several people you know or have read about and giving them all to one character in your story. Only in this way can you be sure of writing interesting characters that will interest both editors and your young readers.

I always keep a pad and pencil handy so I can jot down some extraordinary bit of information about a person I've seen somewhere, and very often this bit of information will be used along with other bits of information for one of the characters I'm developing.

It's very important that you understand the different types of characters for the different age levels. For the early reading levels, the characters are usually simple in their makeup; they become more complex as you go up the age levels. You don't want to develop a character with a myriad of problems for the early reading levels. Older children can handle such characters; in fact, they often seek them out, because they themselves feel that they have more problems than the rest of the world combined. Reading a book on child psychology or child development can give you some ideas as to what common problems are.

The major character or characters in your story must be chosen with extreme care, because the problem of solving the complications of the story will be placed in their hands. They must be capable hands, unless you're writing slapstick, and even then,

192

they must be capable enough to solve the complications by the end of the story.

What sort of main character do you want? The most appropriate main character is one that's neither wholly good nor wholly bad. Of course, the good should outweigh the bad, and the bad points should be chosen with care, because they'll affect the story. Your main character may be lazy or not like to do his homework or have a similar trait. When I use the word *bad*, I'm not making it synonymous with *evil*. I simply mean that the main character has his faults. He is, in other words, normal.

The names of your characters can be very important, because they say a lot about the characters themselves. They must be chosen carefully.

It's also very important that you, the writer, like your major characters, because if you don't, you'll find that it'll be very difficult to write about them. Here's a good example of a likeable character, from Mae Hurley Ashworth's "The Old Lady Next Door":

> *That's what I like about Dave. He isn't as good-looking as some guys, with his long hawk-face and sandy lashes that match his hair, but he has a heart like a marshmallow. You can count on him when your dog gets lost or you need someone to bring you your homework when you have the measles.*

You immediately know a lot about Dave from this passage, and you *like* him!

If you don't like your characters, then I can guarantee you that your readers won't like them, either. I found that in some of my series I began to tire of writing about my major characters, but I still *liked* them. When my major characters were new and fresh, the stories went very fast. After I had tired of them (and this often happens with series characters), it was very difficult for me to create a story around them.

As I've mentioned, you don't have to worry about boys reading stories that have mostly boy characters and girls reading stories that have mostly girl characters. Young people today are more open minded; they simply enjoy interesting characters, whether they're boys or girls.

If you can convince your editor, as I did on several occasions, that your story would make a good start to a series for the magazine, then you have a step up on characterization, because the readers will be familiar with your characters and you won't need to introduce a lot of character information month after month. But there's something else that you have to remember about series characters: They don't normally develop during a series. There'll be some changes, but generally these changes won't be chronological. If your series runs in a magazine for several years, then your main character will be approximately the same age at the end of the series as he was at the beginning. I don't really view this as negative. There's actually something very comforting to young people to know exactly what a character is like. Of course, some things like hair styles, clothing styles, likes and dislikes can change, but nothing major.

A lot of beginning writers act as if adults don't exist in the world of young people. They most certainly do. Remember, though, that if the story has a young protagonist, the adults shouldn't dispense the advice that solves the major complications. Adults are usually in the stories for support, so they, for the most part, should never get in the way.

Above all, in creating your characters, you should create people whom your young readers will enjoy getting to know and whose experiences will entertain them—and perhaps even teach them. You can accomplish this by creating characters whom you yourself would like to meet in real life.

17

Dialogue

Dialogue is important for a number of reasons. Dialogue helps the writer develop the characters of his story. It also makes the reader feel that he's actually taking part in the story, because he's sharing information with the main character. The reader often feels that the main character is talking only to him.

Young readers enjoy listening in on conversations. They like to learn what's happening in the story from the conversations of the main characters, not from the writer's simply telling them the information through narration. Narration is certainly important for transition, but the major scenes in a story should be handled through dialogue.

One of the biggest problems beginning writers have with dialogue is that they make all their characters sound alike. This happens usually because the dialogue is coming from within the writer rather than from within the characters. Even within the same family, each character should sound different. Dialogue can be individualized through word choice, pace, and sentence length.

Dialogue should always sound natural. It should imitate normal speech as closely as possible. If you listen to conversations around you, you'll see that people speak in broken sentences and phrases, use contractions, drop letters, and so on. This, of course, is the extreme, and it's up to you, the writer, to find the middle ground, whereby your characters sound real but are neither so formal that their conversation sounds stilted nor so informal that it's difficult to follow.

Of course, it's easy to say that dialogue must sound natural. In order to sound natural, though, it should probably contain some current slang words, which presents a problem. Slang expressions change almost daily, and if you use many of them, your story will be dated almost before it's out of your typewriter. To solve this problem, you can use some of the timeless slang expressions. If you're still hearing slang expressions that you used years ago, such as "Wow!" or "gee whiz!," chances are they'll be around long after your stories have been in print for a while. Another way of solving this problem is to invent your own slang expressions, like "oosh!," for example, which can mean anything you want it to mean.

You should always keep in mind that geographical background affects the speech of characters. A southerner often has a drawl, a Texan has a twang, and a New Englander has a down-East accent. If you do set your story in a place that has a well-known regional accent, you can use various expressions to make your story ring true. What you're aiming for, remember, is to give your reader the *impression* that your character is from one of these areas. You don't want all of his dialogue to be an exact transcription of the regional accent, because it would be extremely difficult to read. In order to achieve a Southern accent, for instance, I often change *I* to *Ah* and leave off the "t" of the word *just*. This gives the *impression* of a southern accent, while at the same time keeping the dialogue easy to read.

Throughout your story, it's important that the dialogue of your characters seem appropriate to the action and to the characters speaking it. The dialogue must move the story along and must seem in character to the person using it. Your reader must believe that the character would actually talk that way. Here's an example of what I mean, from a "A Horse in the House," by Lee Wyndham. By using somewhat archaic vocabulary and structuring, Ms. Wyndham has reproduced very well the speaking patterns of eighteenth-century American women:

> " 'Tis a pity they do not save their fire for the redcoats instead of fighting among themselves and against the men who are loyal to General Washington," snapped Temperance.
>
> "Judge not too harshly," the mother whispered. "Our War of Independence has been long and weary and the winters are hard on the men. They've had much to bear. Oh, I do wish your father were here." She lapsed into silence and presently drifted off to sleep.

Using foreign languages or foreign accents is handled much the same way in dialogue. Foreign words or expressions should be used only if it's quite clear from the context what they mean. They should be used only for flavor. Various words for *good morning* or *good day* are good to use, because readers can usually understand them quite easily. Changing a "w" to a "v" will usually give the impression that the speaker is German or Russian, and changing a "th" to a "z" will usually give the impression that the speaker is French.

There may be times when you'll want your characters to speak very formal English or to be almost illiterate. In these areas, too, there are certain conventions that you can use. Often, a characteristic way of speaking can be conveyed by a single word or phrase. For the formal speaker, it can be always using the pronoun *I* instead of *me* in the predicate after the verb *to be,* such as "It is I." Even though this form is grammatically correct, it's much too formal for most speakers, and it definitely conveys the impression that the speaker is either well-educated or very pretentious. For the character who's supposed to be illiterate or use very informal English, the word *ain't* is excellent. Not using subject-and-verb agreement, as in *He don't,* can convey the same thing. In this way, most of the rest of the dialogue of the characters can be standard English, and it will still give the *impression,* by the use of these words or phrases, of being either very formal or very informal.

When writing dialogue, you must indent for each new paragraph with each change of speaker. Any gesture or thought or action of the speaker belongs in the same paragraph as his speech. The dialogue itself should be enclosed in double quotation marks; anything quoted within the dialogue should then be enclosed in single quotes. Commas and periods punctuating the sentences of the dialogue should be placed inside quotation marks.

Quotation marks are one of the first things a young reader looks for when he picks up a story. For him, these little signs mean that people are talking about something. He glances at the words between these quotation marks, and if it seems to him they're words that real young people use, he'll read the story.

If dialogue invites a young reader to a page, narration usually repels him. This is another one of the reasons you should use dialogue as much as possible and narration only when necessary.

Unlike in adult stories, in stories for young people, it's necessary to indicate who's just spoken. Young people otherwise lose track of their speakers. But because of this, beginning writers want to use as much variety as possible, and instead of *said*, often indicate dialogue with *replied, answered,* or *spoke,* as well as *yelled, screamed, shouted,* and the like for more vehement speeches. You should avoid doing this. With ordinary statements, you should simply say, "he said." Beginning writers often think that this repetition is boring, but this is a convention that readers accept. In fact, they often don't even notice *said,* except to realize that someone is speaking. Of course, there are times when you *will* need words like *shouted* or *screamed* or *yelled,* especially when you want to indicate that what your character is saying indicates a certain amount of anger, frustration, or other emotion; however, these words should be used sparingly or they will lose their strength.

If you really believe, though, that you have too much repetition of *he said/she said,* then you can use action taglines. For instance: *He turned toward the window. "Has Joe come yet?"*

There are some serious mistakes that beginning writers make when indicating who's speaking a line of dialogue. You should never substitute *laughed* or *sighed* or *smiled* for *said.* These are not verbs of speaking. If you must substitute some other verb of speaking for *said,* use *replied* or *answered* or perhaps *called out.* Never write the following dialogue: *"You'd better not do that," Jason sighed.* People can't *sigh* words—or *smile* them either. Say instead: *Jason sighed. "You'd better not do that," he said.*

It's important for you to remember that dialogue should have a reason for being in a story. It should help move the plot along. When the characters of a story speak, what they say and how they say it should show the reader elements of the story that would be difficult (or too long) to explain with narration.

But if you have your main characters talking for any length of time about things that aren't relevant to the plot, then the story will become dull and uninteresting to the reader. This is where narration comes in—it allows you to show the character moving from place to place. Narration can also add action scenes or description. If your character has what turns out to be a long speech, then instead of using narration, you can interrupt the long speech with questions from the other characters.

How can you, as a beginning writer, achieve an ability to write different types of dialogue? Study people and listen to the way they speak. This can become the model for your characters' dialogue.

When you first meet a person, even before he has opened his mouth to speak, you've formulated the way you think this person might speak. When he opens his mouth, you'll know immediately whether you're right or wrong. The first thing that you notice is the tone of voice. It can be pleasant or unpleasant. The voice quality that you choose for a character in your story should be in keeping with the kind of person you want your character to be.

The next thing you notice about a person speaking is the vocabulary he uses. Is your character using perfect English or imperfect English? Is your character a boy or a girl? Does your character come from a home where standard English is used or where nonstandard English is used? Is your character interested in sports, cars, dolls, or clothes? This information should turn up in your character's vocabulary.

If you've written good dialogue, then something magical happens to your reader, and you, as the author, tend to disappear, and the character comes alive. Your reader isn't reading a story, he's having a conversation with your characters. One of the best tests to determine whether your dialogue is of this caliber is to read it aloud. Does it sound natural? You might also record it on a tape recorder and listen to it over and over, making notes of the changes you want to incorporate. If you feel as though you're too close to the story to be objective, let somebody else (who promises to be objective) read or listen to your dialogue.

If you're still having trouble writing dialogue after all this, then another good source for you to study is a play or a screenplay. I love reading screenplays, and I think they can be extremely helpful in producing good dialogue.

Still another source you can study is the magazine you're considering sending your own story to.

Perhaps the most important thing to remember when writing dialogue in stories for young people is that young people today are so used to the short, snappy sentences they hear on television and in the movies that they'll expect the dialogue of the stories they're reading to be the same way.

18

Titles

A title can be very important in attracting attention to your story. A quotation, a suggestion of suspense, a question, the use of *you* can bring the reader right into the story. Editors often change titles that writers thought were wonderful, but you might find that a really good title will attract an editor and that that editor will let it stand.

Titles should be chosen first of all to attract the eye of the reader. It often happens that the title you've given your story won't appeal to the editor. Do keep in mind that editors have probably been working with titles much longer than you have, so their judgment may be better.

That is not always the case, however. If the title means a lot to you, then by all means fight for it (in a pleasant way). Explain why you think your title would fit the story better. (Don't fight just because they're your words that are being challenged.) If you have a very good reason for wanting to keep a particular title, you might just win.

A title that's both unusual and apt is sometimes very difficult to find. The title should be as accurate as possible. Ask yourself what the central theme of the story is. Is there a particular word that stands out?

The title probably should be as short as possible. Although

some very long titles attract attention, what they mostly attract is irritation on the part of the editor and incomprehension on the part of the young reader. Longer titles, do, however, seem to please young adults, because they think they're funny.

Following are some of the things that you can use to come up with a good title:

1. a pun

2. a literary allusion

3. a rhyme

4. alliteration (which I'll discuss in detail later)

5. the pronoun *you* to appeal directly to the reader

6. a quotation

7. a striking statement

8. an answer to How? What? or Who?

9. the setting of your story

10. time in your story, with the word *minute, hour, day, month,* or *year*

11. the theme of your story

12. a character trait

13. a character's name

If you find that none of these things works for you, then go to various young people's magazines and look at the titles of the short stories. Don't copy them, but use them to stimulate your creativity to come up with your own title. This will also give you some idea of a title that's been acceptable to the editors of this particular magazine.

But sometimes the only right title is a straightforward title that simply tells it like it is. Younger readers usually prefer straightforward titles, such as "My Summer Vacation." Older readers usually prefer titles that are slightly wacky, such as "Leona Ditweiler's Summer Vacation and How She Almost Didn't Recover."

Never underestimate the importance of a good title for your short story. Sometimes if your story is similar in nature to a story written by somebody else, the title will often determine which one will be read first.

You don't usually want to give away too much information in your titles, but sometimes for younger readers, especially if the subject matter is difficult, the title can be a very important clue.

In my minimystery series that ran for several years in *Child Life,* the titles were the most important clues. The young readers didn't know this, however, and could only surmise. If they did indeed pick this up, then I was glad, because it showed that they were reading carefully. That was very important in this series.

I once had a student who told me she wanted very much to be a writer. She really believed that she one day would be a writer. She did in fact write—but all she wrote were *titles,* the titles of the stories she was planning to write one day. She had, she told me, more than 5,000 titles. She was very proud of this accomplishment. And she really believed that one of these days she would get around to writing stories for each one of these titles. I haven't seen her in years, but I doubt very seriously if she's begun to write even one story.

What this girl did do, however, is something that every writer should do—keep a file of titles. Writing titles keeps the mind active. It allows you to build up a storehouse of titles that you might use later for your stories (but of course you have to write those stories!); another thing that it does is start the muses working on possible stories. Many stories have actually come from titles playing around in the writer's head.

Titles come from everywhere, but for many writers, they come out of thin air. If this is the case with you, what you need to do is snatch them up and commit them to paper. Collect titles. Actively write titles. They may develop into stories or they may simply be there for you to choose from the next time you write a story.

Young people will probably like your title for reasons that never occurred to you. They may like a title because it has a certain name in it. (My nine-year-old son readily picks up titles that have his first name in them.) Usually, they like this because it'll tell them whether the story is about a boy or a girl. Or they like the title to tell them whether the story is a mystery, science fiction, romance, or any of the other categories I've discussed.

If your story is a mystery, then the title should promise something mysterious. You could include such a word as *mystery, haunted, ghost, secret, phantom, treasure, the case of,* or *detective* in the title.

If your story is a science fiction story, then it could include such a term as *space ship, planet* (or the name of a particular planet), *asteroid, comet, star, galaxy*—almost any term that you could find in a book about astronomy.

If your story is a romance, then you could include *romance, love, enchantment, true love, tenderness, idol, darling, beloved, dear, fascination, bewitching, fond,* or *devoted,* for instance.

If you're writing a western, then you could choose a word such as *western, gunfight, wagon train, trail, frontier, outlaw, gun, arrow,* or *posse.*

Of course, these are certainly not all of the words that you could use. One of the best ways to find other words that'll fit specific category titles is to look in *Roget's Thesaurus,* which has been an invaluable aid to me over the years.

There are also games that you can play with titles. If you can decide on a suitable noun for a possible title of your story, then you can, by using your knowledge of English structure, play a title-search game.

Let's say that the most important word in a story that you want to write (or that you've already written) is *ghost. Ghost,* then, will be your headword. You can start the game by thinking of all the adjectives that you can use to modify the headword *ghost:*

1. The old ghost

2. The young ghost

3. The happy ghost

4. The sad ghost

5. The good ghost

6. The bad ghost

7. The envious ghost

8. The satisfied ghost

Wait a minute! I like "The Envious Ghost"! I immediately see a story about a ghost who's envious of a young girl or boy, and because of this envy, does mischievous things. Since I've just thought of this story, I'm not quite sure what it is that the ghost is envious of or how the story will be resolved, but maybe you *can*— and maybe you can also get it into print before I can!

Of course, I've used this process to stimulate a story. You can certainly also use this process to bring forth a good title for a story that you've already written. By playing this word game, good titles will come forth. Remember to save for future stories *all* the titles you don't use.

Adjectives, however, aren't the only grammatical elements you can use to try to come up with a good title (or for a good story idea). Prepositional phrases can also modify nouns. Let's take the headword *ghost* and see what we can come up with now:

1. The ghost in the cellar

2. The ghost in the well

3. The ghost in the castle

4. The ghost in the lane

5. The ghost by the lane

6. The ghost in the attic

7. The ghost on the playground

8. The ghost with the green hair

9. The ghost for a day

Well, there are several titles I think I could use, but let's take "The Ghost on the Playground," because I can see a ghost—maybe friendly, maybe unfriendly—haunting a playground; the young people in the story either want to play there all the time because of the ghost or don't want to play there at all because of the ghost. It would depend on whether you want your story to be a funny one, in which a fun ghost haunts a playground because he wants somebody to play with, or a scary one, in which the young people really are afraid to go to the playground.

I also like "The Ghost with Green Hair." It's a title that I think I could develop into a story. It's also a title that I think would attract both editors and readers, because they'd all want to know how in the world a ghost came to have green hair.

Now, let's try developing titles from a basic sentence pattern.

1. The ghost watches through the window

2. The ghost walks softly

3. The ghost came at once

4. The ghost screamed at midnight

5. The ghost wrote the letter

6. The ghost missed the boat

7. The ghost kept guard

Well, finally! I don't really like any of these titles except perhaps the last, "The Ghost Kept Guard." What could a story with this title be about? Well, it certainly tells the reader what to expect, doesn't it? Obviously, the main character can't go someplace that he may want to go because there's a guard ghost keeping him away. But away from what? This is what your reader will want to find out. This is what will make him want to read the story.

In my minimystery series for *Child Life,* the title for the first story, "The Saliva Solution," was a natural, because the solution to the crime was determined by the saliva on the flap of an envelope. It certainly started a very unusual set of circumstances regarding titles, though. The initial title was alliterative, that is, there was a repetition of the initial sounds in the words in the title. I've always liked alliterative titles, and since I happen to know that people like alliteration, I decided to continue using alliterative titles for my other minimysteries. But what happened was that after I'd been writing the minimysteries for several months, I could write an entire minimystery in a matter of hours—but it would take me days to determine a good alliterative title! I'd pore over the thesaurus, trying to find just the right words. I once tried to stop using alliteration and sent in a nonalliterative title for a story, but one of the editors changed it to an acceptable alliterative title. In other words, alliteration had become an integral part of the minimystery series.

In the early part of the minimystery series, the subject matter dealt with forensic science. Some of the other titles were "A Hint of Hair" and "A Grain of Guilt." But a change in editorial policy forced all the stories to be health-related, so the new titles had to reflect this slant. "The Transfusion Transfer" and "The Lactic Liability" are a couple of examples. I found it very difficult to come up with titles after this editorial change, but I was locked into the alliteration pattern.

When I developed the Dr. Phobia series for *Jack and Jill*, I was still smarting from the difficulty I was having with the titles for the minimystery series, so I tried to make sure that creating titles for the new series would be easier. I thought that since Dr. Phobia was a psychiatrist and that since visits to him would probably be kept secret (inasmuch as young people don't like to let other young people know they're seeking professional help for their problems), a very good title for each story in the series would simply be "Dr. Phobia—Secret Case File No. 1," ". . . No. 2," ". . . No. 3," and so on. This was acceptable to the editors, for, after all, it had the attractive word *secret* in it. And it solved a lot of problems in that the titles were ready made. After coming up with the first title, I didn't have to worry about titles for the rest of the series. Very seldom does one have that kind of luck!

For the Allison Graham series in *Health Explorer*, which was also a health-related adventure, I wanted suspense/adventure words. Two of the titles were "Escape Across the Chari" and "Invasion of Port Elizabeth." Most of the titles mentioned geographical places and included a suspense/adventure word.

For the Toby Torrance series in *Jr. Medical Detective,* I used "The Case of . . ." in all the titles. "The Case of the Serious Sunburn" and "The Case of the Deadly Cold" were two titles in the series. Frankly, I wasn't too happy with these titles, either, but they fit the subject, which is easily seen as health-related. Further, they had the word *case* in them, which attracted readers interested in mysteries who might otherwise have been turned off by the subject matter. They were indeed mysteries with clues throughout the story that the reader (and the main characters) could use to solve the case.

For the Microscope Morris series, also in *Jr. Medical Detective,* but written under the name Stan Edwards, I used the word *caper* in all the titles. I thought that word fit the light and humorous mood of these stories, although now that I look back on it, *caper* probably isn't all that common a word to young people. Some of these titles had forensic science elements; others simply mentioned the setting. They were actually a hodge-podge of information taken from the stories, but they were all descriptive of what was taking place. Examples of these titles are "The Inky River Clue Caper" and "The Creepy Clothes Caper."

One final note: You really shouldn't worry about a title until you've finished your story (unless, of course, you're using the title to help stimulate a story). A lot of beginning writers spend hours and hours worrying about a title, even before they've written one word. If you absolutely have to have a title for a story before you can proceed, then by all means make a distinction between a *working* title and a *final* title.

19

Preparing the Final Manuscript

All magazine story manuscripts submitted to legitimate magazine publishers are read, except those that are handwritten. But there's a proper form that a manuscript should take, and it's to your advantage that your manuscript look as professional as possible. Here are the guidelines that you should follow when you submit your manuscript:

You should use a good weight of paper, 8½" by 11". Use a good grade of white bond. Don't use erasable paper—it smudges too easily.

Your manuscript should be neatly typed. Any pages that contain strike-overs should be retyped. You should have as few erasures as possible.

You should submit the original of your manuscript to the editor and keep a copy (preferably a photocopy) for yourself.

WRITING SHORT STORIES FOR YOUNG PEOPLE

     Each page of the manuscript should be numbered in the top right-hand corner, except the first page, which isn't numbered.

     You should indicate on every page (except the first page) your last name in the left-hand corner.

     The format of the first page should conform to the following specifications:

Your name   Approximately so many words

Your address

Your city, state, ZIP code

Your telephone number(s)

TITLE IN ALL CAPS
(halfway down the page)

by

Your Name

     Your story begins here (three-fourths of the way down the page).

PREPARING THE FINAL MANUSCRIPT

I myself use a 1½-inch margin around each page of a manuscript. This leaves the editor plenty of room for comments, and it looks nice besides. I don't understand why so many beginning writers insist on typing from one edge of the paper to the other and from the top to the bottom—single spaced! Make sure you don't do this!

At the top right-hand side of the first page, you should include the approximate number of words in your story, rounded off. Generally, a page will contain approximately 20-25 typed lines, giving you approximately 200-250 words per page. To determine how many words you've written, you don't count every word on the page. What you do is count the number of letters and spaces on an average line and then divide by 5. This will give you the approximate number of words you've typed on each line. The answer will generally be 10, but whatever number it is, multiply it by the number of lines per page, which will usually be 20-25, giving you 200-250 words. (If you have more words than this on your page, then you probably have too many. The best-looking page usually has 200 words on it—10 words per line and 20 lines per page.) You should then find out the maximum number of words acceptable to whatever publication you're writing your story for. Into this number you should divide the number of words per page, and you'll have the number of typed pages you'll be allowed for your story. If the publication has a 500-word maximum for short stories and you generally type 200 words per page, then your story may be no more than 2½ pages long. That may not seem very long to you, but that's the maximum length this particular publication will accept. Remember, however, that the editor is looking for *approximate* length. After you've been writing for a while, you'll find that you'll be able to gear your writing to a certain number of pages quite easily. Until you reach that point, however, you may have to do a lot of adding or cutting of words.

If the publication you're sending the story to has listed an acceptable maximum length for stories, then you should make sure you've maintained this length. Don't think that because you've written an excellent short story exceeding this maximum length, the number of words you've written will be overlooked.

There are many reasons for this length requirement that have nothing whatsoever to do with how good the story is. Don't send a story to an editor and say, "I know your guidelines say that you accept only stories with a maximum of 500 words, but this is such an excellent story that I thought you'd want to consider it, even though it has 1,000 words." It will be sent right back to you.

Actually, I've found that cutting a too-long story can actually enhance the dramatic impact and continuity. If it's only a matter of cutting a few hundred words, then reread the manuscript word for word, cutting out anything that's unnecessary. If you're honest with yourself (and not one of those writers who think that every word they've written is immortal), then you'll be able to find enough words to cut. I've often cut stories in half, leaving out characters and whole scenes, without damaging the stories. You can often give one character's actions and dialogue to another character, for instance—an enormous aid in cutting.

If your problem is a too-short story, then your job will be easier. Don't pad, however. Don't add unnecessary information just to get the correct length. Adding words to your short story must be done right. Strengthen the characters. Expand their motivations for doing what they do. Add more complications, and expand the ones you already have. Elaborate on the setting. Replace some of the bare dialogue with full dialogue. You might even find with this expansion that you'll need some new minor or stock characters.

Here's a method I've often used for cutting (I've also used this method when putting together the final manuscript): I cut the manuscript up into scenes and then spread these scenes out on a long table. Then I sort and resort, arrange and rearrange, until I feel that I have the scenes in the correct order (yes, I know this is what a word processor can do). Then I tape them onto new sheets of paper. Next, I read through the story, penciling in the corrections I want to make, and finally, I start typing. As I'm typing, I often think of new things I want to add, usually in the form of transitions, until I have a clean copy. I've found that I edit well only if I'm working with a clean copy. I can do gross editing (major editing) from a rougher copy, but I need a clean copy for fine editing, that is, smoothing out the little rough spots.

A professional-looking manuscript suggests that you, too, are a professional—and that's what you want to be, isn't it, a *professional* writer? So your final manuscript must be neatly typed. I'd suggest you use pica, although I've had a number of editors tell me they really don't mind receiving manuscripts typed in elite. Most editors, however, don't like fancy types, like italic or script. If you use a word processor, don't use a dot-matrix printer that's not *really* letter quality, as it's difficult to read. Don't use justified right margins, as this is difficult to read, too.

For copies, I use photocopies. I never use carbon copies, and I frankly don't think that many other writers do these days, either. It's just too much bother, and the little extra cost of the photocopy is worth it. It's a good idea to have at least two copies of your manuscript, but you most definitely have to have one!

A lot of beginning writers want to know about using pseudonyms. I've used two in my children's stories, but I used them only at the request of an editor. He didn't want to have two stories with the same byline in one magazine. I didn't use them for anonymity. I use pseudonyms for some of my adult stories, again not for anonymity, but for association. I want my real name to be associated with my children's stories, because I write mostly children's stories. If you think that a problem would develop for you or for your family if you wrote under your real name, then by all means use a pseudonym, but frankly, one of the thrills of writing is seeing your *real* name in print.

Don't type on the front page of your manuscript such remarks as "For Sale" or "Usual Rights." The editor knows that the manuscript is for sale, and the rights requested are set by company policy.

Don't bind a manuscript in any way. Don't staple or pin the pages together. Use a paper clip.

If your short story is no more than four or five pages long, then it's considered perfectly acceptable for you to fold it in thirds like a business letter and to send it in a large business-sized envelope.

If your short story is 12-15 pages long, then you may fold it in half and send it in a 7″ by 10″ manila envelope.

If your short story is 15 or more pages, then it *must* be sent flat in a 10″ by 13″ manila envelope.

But I must confess that I send *all* of my stories flat, no matter how many pages they are.

With each short story, I send an envelope of the same size, stamped and addressed to myself, folded in half, and inserted into the mailing envelope along with the story. This is known as a SASE, a self-addressed, stamped envelope.

Don't turn one of the pages of your short story upside down or over to be able to discover when it's returned whether it was read or not. Editors hate this and will immediately dislike you. Your manuscript will be read—at least as far as the editor thinks it needs to be read.

Don't worry about copyright if your story is to be published in a copyrighted publication. Copyright here is automatic. (I'll discuss selling or retaining rights to your stories in the next chapter.) If, however, your story is to be published in an uncopyrighted publication, such as a church bulletin, an uncopyrighted literary magazine, or a handout passed out in school, then your copyright can be forfeited and your work enter into the public domain unless you yourself get it copyrighted. You can do this by obtaining forms for official copyright from the Library of Congress in Washington, D.C.

Don't worry about piracy—you're wasting valuable energy if you do. Many beginning writers think that all editors are out to steal their stories. Actually stories are too common, even ones dealing with the same subject matter, for an editor to be interested in stealing yours. No reputable magazine publisher would ever steal your work, and no disreputable magazine publisher would stay in business long enough for you to worry about it.

What if you sent your manuscript out and it comes back with a rejection slip? Don't get depressed. A rejection slip really does mean generally that your short story wasn't right for a certain publication. Anyway, you should be so excited about the current story that you're working on that a rejection will only be a minor irritation. Send the story out again—the same day!—and get back to work on your current masterpiece.

If the editor who sent your story back has made some comment on the rejection slip, then by all means keep sending stories to that editor. No editor is going to take the time to comment on a story unless he believes the author shows promise. Take all editorial comments seriously.

It's an incredible thrill for a writer to receive a letter or a telephone call from an editor accepting a story. But almost always with this letter or telephone call comes a suggestion for revisions, and here we get back to manuscript preparation. Editorial-revision suggestions can vary from changing a confusing word to rewriting a story entirely. I've heard some horror stories about writers who've refused to change even one word of their manuscripts and ended up not getting published anywhere. I've heard other horror stories of writers who got letters from editors asking for revisions, to which the writer would agree, only to put off doing the revisions, pleading that other things got in the way. Let me tell you something very important: This isn't the way it works! If you're a serious writer, and if an editor writes you or calls you and asks for revisions, then you should make them. Now, of course, if there are specific instances of things that you think shouldn't be changed, then you should discuss those with the editor. All good editors will listen to you, and you might even be able to make points.

What I mean is that if an editor has taken the time to talk to you or write to you about your manuscript, he's interested. He's not just killing time, because frankly, he doesn't have time to kill! What you need to remember is that the editor thinks your manuscript is good enough to save. *But it's not the only publishable manuscript out there!* Believe me, if you don't heed the editor's words, then there are hundreds of other writers out there just waiting for their chance to work with this particular editor. The editor was being a professional when he contacted you about working on your manuscript. You should in turn be a professional about doing the revisions. The results of this professionalism, of course, will be that you'll be a *published* writer.

20
Markets

Now that you've finished the final draft of your short story, the next step is to send it out for publication. A careful examination of the markets is a must. You can usually find a good selection of young people's magazines at your public library. Do they publish short stories similar to the one you've just written? If they do, study them! If they don't, you can find information about other magazines for young people in *Writer's Market* and *Fiction Writer's Market,* which will give you most of the information you need to determine whether or not a publication will be receptive to your story. These two books can be purchased in almost any bookstore, or they can usually be found on reserve at your public library and consulted for free.

If possible, you should send your story to a specific editor by name. This is very important. The names of the editors of magazines are found in *Writer's Market* and *Fiction Writer's Market,* as well as in the magazines themselves. I can't stress enough how important it is that you send your story to a *name* and not simply to "The Editor." It shows the editor that you cared enough to find out who actually edits the magazine.

It isn't at all necessary for you to submit a cover letter with a magazine story; however, if you feel you must, by all means keep it short and don't say, "I'm sending you a story for possible publication." The editor already knows this. Your letter should include information that you think is important for the editor to know. If you have some publishing credits, include them. Editors are always interested in knowing if somebody else has taken a chance on you. This works both ways, though. Magazines like to have *published* writers within their pages, but editors also like to discover *new* writers.

One thing your cover letter should *never* do is try to explain your story. If the idea doesn't come through in reading the story itself, then you'll probably need to rewrite it.

If you're not a professional illustrator, don't include illustrations with your manuscript. The number of people who worry about this is absolutely incredible. A beginning writer often spends months searching for the perfect illustrator, paying that person good money for often less-than-professional illustrations, and then submitting these illustrations with his story. What you need to remember is that who illustrates your story is the prerogative of the editor. It's not something that you need to worry about. In fact, I love wondering just exactly how my characters will look after the illustrator has drawn them. I really have never been disappointed, although there have been many occasions when the illustrator didn't draw my characters the way I had initially visualized them. It's not even a good idea for you to indicate in your story where you think there should be illustrations. The artist usually decides that, with perhaps some suggestions from the editor.

Magazine publishers usually won't acknowledge having received your manuscript, but if you enclose a post card, they might return it to let you know that your story has indeed arrived at its destination.

Generally, if you haven't heard from the editor after about two months, you're perfectly within your rights to inquire about your short story. (This response time varies from publication to publication, so you should always check the market listings.) Your inquiry should be done by letter. If this doesn't work, then I suggest a second letter, perhaps a little more tersely written. And finally, if all else fails, I suggest a telephone call.

217

Although submitting the same short story to several different publishers at the same time is considered acceptable, especially by many religious publications, I'm totally against it. In fact, many editors have told me that they find it difficult to give their total attention to a story if they know it's a multiple submission. I realize that getting a manuscript published takes a lot of time, but one way to avoid feeling that you're getting nothing accomplished is to continue writing. If you do submit the same short story to several different publishers, you should by all means tell them that you're doing so. Not to do this is dishonest and could in fact cause you a lot of trouble. If, for instance, two or more publications accept the manuscript, then you're going to have to let someone know that he can't publish it. And I can guarantee you that your name will be remembered at that particular publishing house and that it'll be a long, long time before any of your stories will again be considered for publication there—if ever!

Most magazines for young people pay on publication. They may also hold your story for a considerable length of time before either printing it or returning it. When you're choosing a publication to send your story to, choose the one that indicates that it'll return your story in the shortest possible time and then work down toward the longest, unless you particularly like a publication and are prepared to wait. Of course, everybody likes the idea of being paid on acceptance (and frankly, I think this is more fair to the writer), but I also think that in the beginning it's much more important to be published than it is to worry about when you'll get the money for your story. Now, I know that this is going to make a lot of my writer-friends angry at me, but you first have to consider what arrangement is best for *you*. You must develop a track record. This means numbers. If you submit your stories to only publications that pay on acceptance, then it'll take you a long time to develop a track record. Just keep in mind that if you're being published, you'll eventually reach a point at which you will not only be paid on acceptance of a manuscript, you'll also often be paid *before a manuscript is even written!* It just takes time, and this is something that you, the beginning writer, must be willing to accept. You must be willing to let your writing career evolve. Don't

218

start out thinking that you'll become the darling of the publishing world overnight. Oh, well, you can start out thinking that if you want to—just don't start acting like it!

I'd like to say a few words here about selling all rights to your stories, because most magazines for young people do buy all rights. I've sold all rights to most of my short stories for young people. It has never bothered me to do so. I suppose that's because I'm a very prolific writer. I write fast, and I write a lot. I find writing easy. (It's the *rewriting* that takes the time!) It never has been difficult for me to write a short story or to create new short story characters. When I was selling all rights to my stories, what I had in mind was establishing a track record.

You might be able to retain rights to a story (or *regain* rights, as Ivy Ruckman did with her "Melba the Brain" stories) and then sell second rights, for instance, for a collection of your short stories; but so few juvenile short story collections by individual authors are published that I don't think it's worth worrying about. You might also want to develop a novel from a short story you've published. There would be no problem with your doing this, provided the publication you sold the story to doesn't own the rights to the characters you've developed (and that is seldom the case). Even if they do, however, most publications are usually willing to reassign one-time rights to you for just such a purpose as writing a novel. Anyway, I don't know one editor who cares whether or not you've sold all rights to what you've written. But I know a lot of editors who are interested in what you've published.

While I still write short stories, I also write books. Very seldom do editors buy all rights to books. I own my books. The amount of money I could have gained from retaining rights to my short stories (provided I could have sold them in the first place!) is minuscule compared to what I've gained by having published as many short stories for young people as I have. The most important accomplishment is what you're reading now, *Writing Short Stories for Young People!*

My advice to you is this: Get published! Don't worry about whether or not a magazine buys all rights to your stories. Unless you have a definite commitment from a television or motion picture producer, then just what do you think you're going to do with that story?

If, however, you still don't like the idea of selling all rights to your short stories, then submit them only to magazines that indicate that they buy *first North American serial rights*. This means that the publisher has the right to print the story once.

Some of the best markets for your short stories may be in English-language markets other than those in the United States. *The Writers' and Artists' Yearbook* lists the names and addresses of markets for short stories for young people in England, Scotland, Ireland, Canada, Australia, New Zealand, South Africa, India, and Pakistan. You may not want to try these markets first, but if you don't have any luck placing your story in American markets, then you may find receptive editors abroad. Always send your manuscript by airmail and include international reply coupons (purchased at your local post office) paper-clipped to your SASE.

And now, a word about agents. I have an agent, and she's a very good one. In fact, I don't think I could do without her. But she handles my books; she doesn't handle my short stories. *You don't need an agent to sell your short stories for young people.* In any case, agents rarely handle short stories, even adult short stories, because it isn't worth their time (and time really is money!). Also, if you're a beginning writer, it would be difficult to get an agent anyway, because you have to prove yourself first. It really is true that the best way to get an agent is to prove that you don't really need one. And the best way to do this is to know your markets well enough that the first one you send your short story to will publish it.

If I've made becoming a writer sound like hard work, then I've been successful. Writing takes a lot of time and serious effort on your part. But if you stay with it, you'll keep getting better and better.

By now, you've probably decided what category of short story you want to write—mystery, suspense/adventure, science fiction, fantasy, historical, western, romance, or religious; perhaps you may even want to try your hand at a mainstream. You've probably also decided the age level you want to write for, and you may even have written character bios for your major and minor characters. You may also have chosen a title. If you're not at this point yet, then turn back to the beginning of this book and start reading again. If you are, then close this book and start writing that short story!

Index

INDEX

INDEX

INDEX

Other Books of Interest

General Writing Books

Beginning Writer's Answer Book, edited by Kirk Polking (paper) $12.95
Getting the Words Right: How to Revise, Edit and Rewrite, by Theodore A. Rees Cheney $14.95
How to Get Started in Writing, by Peggy Teeters (paper) $8.95
How to Increase Your Word Power, by the editors of Reader's Digest $19.95
How to Write a Book Proposal, by Michael Larsen $9.95
How to Write While You Sleep, by Elizabeth Ross $14.95
Just Open a Vein, edited by William Brohaugh $15.95
Knowing Where to Look: The Ultimate Guide to Research, by Lois Horowitz $18.95
Law & the Writer, edited by Polking & Meranus (paper) $10.95
Make Every Word Count, by Gary Provost (paper) $7.95
Pinckert's Practical Grammar, by Robert C. Pinckert $14.95
Teach Yourself to Write, by Evelyn Stenbock (paper) $9.95
The 29 Most Common Writing Mistakes & How to Avoid Them, by Judy Delton $9.95
Writer's Block & How to Use It, by Victoria Nelson $14.95
The Writer's Digest Guide to Manuscript Formats, by Buchman & Groves $16.95
Writer's Encyclopedia, edited by Kirk Polking (paper) $16.95
Writer's Guide to Research, by Lois Horowitz $9.95
Writer's Market, edited by Glenda Neff $21.95
Writing for the Joy of It, by Leonard Knott $11.95

Nonfiction Writing

Basic Magazine Writing, by Barbara Kevles $16.95
How to Sell Every Magazine Article You Write, by Lisa Collier Cool $14.95
How to Write & Sell the 8 Easiest Article Types, by Helene Schellenberg Barnhart $14.95
Writing Creative Nonfiction, by Theodore A. Rees Cheney $15.95
Writing Nonfiction that Sells, by Samm Sinclair Baker $14.95

Fiction Writing

Creating Short Fiction, by Damon Knight (paper) $8.95
Fiction is Folks: How to Create Unforgettable Characters, by Robert Newton Peck (paper) $8.95
Fiction Writer's Market, edited by Laurie Henry $18.95
Handbook of Short Story Writing, by Dickson and Smythe (paper) $8.95
How to Write & Sell Your First Novel, by Oscar Collier with Frances Spatz Leighton $14.95
How to Write Short Stories that Sell, by Louise Boggess (paper) $7.95
One Way to Write Your Novel, by Dick Perry (paper) $7.95
Storycrafting, by Paul Darcy Boles (paper) $9.95
Writing the Novel: From Plot to Print, by Lawrence Block (paper) $8.95

Special Interest Writing Books

The Children's Picture Book: How to Write It, How to Sell It, by Ellen E.M. Roberts (paper) $14.95
Comedy Writing Secrets, by Melvin Helitzer $16.95
The Complete Book of Scriptwriting, by J. Michael Straczynski (paper) $9.95
The Craft of Comedy Writing, by Sol Saks $14.95
The Craft of Lyric Writing, by Sheila Davis $18.95
Guide to Greeting Card Writing, edited by Larry Sandman (paper) $8.95

How to Make Money Writing Fillers, by Connie Emerson (paper) $8.95
How to Sell & Re-Sell Your Writing, by Duane Newcomb $10.95
How to Write a Cookbook and Get It Published, by Sara Pitzer $15.95
How to Write & Sell A Column, by Raskin & Males $10.95
How to Write and Sell Your Personal Experiences, by Lois Duncan (paper) $9.95
How to Write and Sell (Your Sense of) Humor, by Gene Perret (paper) $9.95
How to Write Tales of Horror, Fantasy & Science Fiction, edited by J.N. Williamson $15.95
How to Write the Story of Your Life, by Frank P. Thomas $14.95
How You Can Make $50,000 a Year as a Nature Photojournalist, by Bill Thomas (paper) $17.95
Mystery Writer's Handbook, by The Mystery Writers of America (paper) $9.95
Nonfiction for Children: How to Write It, How to Sell It, by Ellen E.M. Roberts $16.95
On Being a Poet, by Judson Jerome $14.95
The Poet's Handbook, by Judson Jerome (paper) $8.95
Poet's Market, by Judson Jerome $17.95
Successful Outdoor Writing, by Jack Samson $11.95
Travel Writer's Handbook, by Louise Zobel (paper) $10.95
TV Scriptwriter's Handbook, by Alfred Brenner (paper) $9.95
Writing After 50, by Leonard L. Knott $12.95
Writing for Children & Teenagers, by Lee Wyndham (paper) $9.95
Writing Short Stories for Young People, by George Edward Stanley $15.95
Writing the Modern Mystery, by Barbara Norville $15.95

The Writing Business

A Beginner's Guide to Getting Published, edited by Kirk Polking $10.95
Complete Guide to Self-Publishing, by Tom & Marilyn Ross $19.95
Freelance Jobs for Writers, edited by Kirk Polking (paper) $8.95
How to Bulletproof Your Manuscript, by Bruce Henderson $9.95
How to Get Your Book Published, by Herbert W. Bell $15.95
How to Understand and Negotiate a Book Contract or Magazine Agreement, by Richard Balkin $11.95
How to Write Irresistible Query Letters, by Lisa Collier Cool $10.95
How You Can Make $25,000 a Year Writing (No Matter Where You Live), by Nancy Edmonds Hanson $15.95
Literary Agents: How to Get & Work with the Right One for You, by Michael Larsen $9.95
Professional Etiquette for Writers, by William Brohaugh $9.95

To order directly from the publisher, include $2.00 postage and handling for 1 book and 50¢ for each additional book. Allow 30 days for delivery.

Writer's Digest Books, Department B
1507 Dana Avenue, Cincinnati, Ohio 45207
Credit card orders call TOLL-FREE
1-800-543-4644 (Outside Ohio)
1-800-551-0884 (Ohio only)
Prices subject to change without notice.

For information on how to receive Writer's Digest Books at special Book Club member prices, please write to:

Promotion Manager
Writer's Digest Book Club
1507 Dana Avenue
Cincinnati, Ohio 45207